Dedicated to...

The animals and my family and my friends and every source
of inspiration. Oh, and good dark chocolate.

The essays contained herein were written between 2009 and 2013, and all first appeared in the blog, *Vegan Feminist Agitator* on Blogger.com

For information regarding permission, contact the author at marla@marlarose.com.

ISBN 1490462295

ISBN-13: 978-1490462295

Acknowledgements

Thank you to all who have stuck with my weird little blog from the early days until now. Let's have Indian food together, okay?

And nothing would happen without John Beske. The smartest thing I ever did was decide to date a nice guy. I can say without a doubt, you are the very best.

If you like what you see and read here, please consider following Vegan Feminist Agitator by visiting
VeganFeministAgitator.com

and follow Marla's other writings and exploits on
VeganStreet.com

VivianSharpe.com

MarlaRose.com

WHEN VEGANS (ALMOST) RULE THE WORLD

Table of Contents

WHEN VEGANS (ALMOST) RULE THE WORLD

Introduction

Marla feels your pain. When your refusal to partake in Aunt Edna's tuna casserole leads to a spirited discussion about the evolution of our powerful canine teeth, the certainty that plants feel pain and fear death, and the delightful deliciousness of bacon, Marla knows what you're going through. She's been there.

When every single one of your omnivorous friends insists that they're protecting the environment and animal welfare because the only meat they consume is the product of happy animals that lived long and pampered lives, Marla is there to point out that all the "happy meat" in the country (specious as that term is) would barely keep the city of Des Moines in burgers.

And if you like to eat animals and you can't understand why vegans have to be so uppity about it all the time, well, Marla cares about you too. She might mock you, but she'll do it with love, and in the end, she'll do it to protect you from looking like an idiot. You see, a lot of things omnivores say in their arguments with vegans are, you have to admit, really stupid, and a less sensitive vegan may really start to doubt your intelligence, and then decide she can do your job better than you can, and then there you are, out on the street, and in this economy!

No, Marla doesn't want you to lose your job. She'll just gently point out the foolishness of your argument and then encourage you to either come up with a better one (even though this is pointless, because there has never been an anti-vegan argument that hasn't been thoroughly blown out of the water), or accept that the vegans are right and then either join them or at least let them be.

Better yet, you should simply read this book and the blog that inspired it.

Marla started writing *Vegan Feminist Agitator* in late 2007, because it is sometimes hard to be a vegan – not because there isn't a plethora of luscious vegan foods (there most certainly is) or a warm and inviting vegan community (that exists as well, and if you don't know where to look, Marla will help you find it or co-create it) – but because it's frustrating that so many otherwise intelligent and compassionate people just don't get it.

Marla understands why people don't get it, and she's using every tool in her mighty belt to make sure the message sinks in.

The most powerful of these tools are her rapier of satire that tears through the veils of complacency that prevent people from seeing the naked artifice of the Emporer's argument, and her compass of compassion that guides the reader to the beautiful day when vegans (almost) rule the world.

Each of the 31 essays that follow is a gem of wisdom designed to expose the ridiculousness of thought that supports a system that blinds the world to the suffering and destruction of the industries that exploit animals. Like other great satirists, Marla can make people laugh at their own foolishness, and most of these pieces are genuinely funny and fun to read.

But this rapier has a sharp point, and Marla's not afraid to use it. Those who get on the wrong side of the debate will get skewered (as her husband, I can personally attest to this). She has enough rage under the surface to fuel a movement. And that's exactly what she's doing.

Marla is a voice for the age. She's providing a welcome and essential voice of wit and humor to a subject that genuinely needs it. Follow her, and she'll lead you down the path to Global Vegan Domination.

Resist her, and prepare to be mocked.

-John Beske

When Vegans (Almost) Rule the World
originally posted April 26, 2012

When vegans (almost) rule the world, vegan nutritionists will be consulted on mainstream news stories about omnivorous diets. They will look very concerned and, while saying that it might be possible to not die prematurely as an omnivore, those people should be very careful with their meal planning.

When vegans (almost) rule the world, omnivores will complain amongst themselves about all the photos their herbivorous friends upload onto Facebook of their animal-free food. "Ugh, do I need to see this all the time?" they will say. "Is there no safe haven?"

When vegans (almost) rule the world, expectant omnivorous parents will be asked, "Well, I understand that you eat animal products, but you're not planning to force that upon your child, are you?"

When vegans (almost) rule the world, omnivores will dread every Thanksgiving. They will have to get together with their vegan relatives and sit silently as dish after dish is served, not even a piece of turkey or anything else from an animal on the table. They will wish that on a holiday, they could just be accepted for who they are.

When vegans (almost) rule the world, meat-eaters will have to eat the foul, cobbled together Omnivore Plate at weddings.

When vegans (almost) rule the world, once identified as meat-eaters, omnivores will have to listen to stories from co-workers about "the cousin of a friend of my neighbor whose son was dating an omnivore and she got really sick and died" and that sort of thing.

When vegans (almost) rule the world, the best chefs will roll their eyes at omnivorous requests. "I cannot work with such inferior ingredients," they will say. "Those with boring, unsophisticated palates and extreme limitations shouldn't come to my restaurant expecting to eat."

When vegans (almost) rule the world, omnivores will be irritated by how they are depicted on television ("So stereotypic!") and they will be crushed when their favorite meat-eating celebrities jump ship and start promoting veganism. "It just makes us all look flaky."

When vegans (almost) rule the world, it will be implied that omnivores are pushy and out-of-touch when they try to defend their eating habits.

When vegans (almost) rule the world, omnivorous parents will worry that their children's packed lunches don't look appetizing. They will also hope that their children's lunches don't draw too much negative attention to them.

When vegans (almost) rule the world, omnivores will be bitterly disappointed when they discover that their carry-out food has vegetables all over it and no meat.

When vegans (almost) rule the world, smart phones will have special apps to help omnivores find the restaurants that serve meat.

When vegans (almost) rule the world, omnivores will be competitive with each other over how long they've been omnivorous and judge one another for their motivations for eating meat.

When vegans (almost) rule the world, meat-eaters will hear stories from people at parties about how they used to be omnivorous but they had to quit because it was just too hard. Plus, they felt too weak and sickly.

WHEN VEGANS (ALMOST) RULE THE WORLD

When vegans (almost) rule the world, omnivores will feel uncomfortable when people stare at their food with a mixture of disgust and morbid curiosity. "Ew! What was that?" people will say.

When vegans (almost) rule the world, it will be implied that men who are omnivores are wimps and women who are omnivores are on crazy diets. Never mind. When vegans (almost) rule the world, we'll be done with that nonsense.

When vegans (almost) rule the world, meat-eaters will lament the lack of positive role models and wish that they didn't publicly embarrass each other all the time. Omnivores who argue with each other are accused of "hurting the movement."

When vegans (almost) rule the world, when two meat-eaters get married, their friends will ask, "You're not going to have an omnivorous wedding, are you?"

When vegans (almost) rule the world, omnivores will be derided for eating mock tofu and faux tempeh and they will be told that no one understands why they'd want to eat an imitation of something that they supposedly don't like. It will be implied that they are clearly stifling their inner-vegan.

When vegans (almost) rule the world, some omnivores will be told that they look healthy despite their habits.

When vegans (almost) rule the world, when groups of omnivores and vegans go out to eat together, the omnivores just know that they will have to suffer through some half-assed meal by a chef who doesn't know how to cook "their" food.

When vegans (almost) rule the world, it will be implied that omnivores must have a ton of willpower to live the way that they do.

When vegans (almost) rule the world, omnivores will meet each other through the website MeatyDate.com.

When vegans (almost) rule the world, whenever omnivores adopt a dog or cat, they will be asked what they will feed them.

When vegans (almost) rule the world, it will be assumed that any ailment or injury an omnivore has is directly linked to that person's diet.

When vegans (almost) rule the world, it will be implied that omnivores are hypocrites if they wear non-leather shoes.

When vegans (almost) rule the world, omnivores will roll their eyes every time someone asks them where they get their fiber.

When vegans (almost) rule the world, omnivores will always be accused of having an agenda.

When vegans (almost) rule the world, it will be implied that omnivores are uptight, inhibited puritans, chomping on dead bodies, ovum and secretions, when it's clear that luscious fruits and vegetables are what the sexy people eat.

When vegans (almost) rule the world, omnivores will be told collectively to get a life.

WHEN VEGANS (ALMOST) RULE THE WORLD

Veganism, Feminism, Integration
Originally posted on Wednesday, February 24, 2010

Ever since I was old enough to form a self-aware thought, I was a feminist. More accurately, I was a pre-feminist: feminism implies, at least to me, that there is something in the world that feminists are responding to: inequality, injustice, fewer opportunities, something bad. As a young child, I was blissfully unaware that there were even those who considered anything but absolute shoulder-to-shoulder equality. Thankfully, I grew up before Disney had princessified girlhood, thus it never occurred to me to aspire to being such a creature. Like the other daughters of second wave feminism, I would go wherever my myriad electrifying passions took me. My Barbie proxy figure hung out at the beach with Skipper and Ken from time to time, but she also traveled the world as a high-stakes business woman and volunteered as a veterinarian and rescued horses from equine-oppressing dolls with evil eyebrows drawn in with a ball point pen. My desk drawers were messily stuffed with the loose papers upon which I mapped out my future: what my house would look like (there was always an indoor pool in the basement), stories about the mysteries I would solve, the secret worlds I would discover. Why would I think anything wasn't available to me? I believed that I was born into a benevolent matriarchal dictatorship with my grandmother as good-natured empress and everyone else falling into line behind her. Though the women in my family pulled the strings to make their units function well, they had to keep up appearances that their marriages were egalitarian to be nice. This was all just for appearances, I was certain. I extrapolated it to become my earliest interpretation of women in the world.

And then the real world started trickling in. I would watch All In The Family and wonder what that Archie Bunker character was talking about anyway, always mocking the "women libbers" on the show. He was just stupid, right? But Edith, his wife, would greet Archie at the door, as endlessly sunny as Archie was scowling. Why was she subservient to anyone, let alone such a grouch? And what was this Equal Rights Amendment, anyway, the thing that was making everyone so upset on the news? Why was something like the ERA even necessary? Of course we were equal. Whoever thought otherwise? Lots of people, it turned out. I started to notice that the principal and superintendents at school were always men. All the presidents were men, too. Nixon, Ford, Carter, Reagan and all the men around them: one after the next, like a row of mechanical ducks at the carnival game. I saw my mother, hardly an avowed feminist, derided by the fathers at the Little League games when she was coach of my brother's team, the only female coach in the league, time and time again. I remember one opposing coach telling my mother that she was out of her element, that she should join the PTA instead. My mother didn't skip a beat when she informed him that she was also president of the PTA, her arms folded in front of her chest, just short of saying, "And what have you done lately?" He stormed off in a huff, I remember the cloud of dust puffing up behind him, as my mother savored the moment before she resumed her coaching. The battles she couldn't win at home, she would win on the field.

Watching my mother and her friends and the world around me, my natural response was to become a feminist. It was as intuitive to me as turning on the light when you're trying to see in a dark room. Of course! It was the same thing when I became a vegetarian at fifteen. It was utterly natural, putting my beliefs into practice. My feminism and my veganism grow from the same seed, even from the same root. They have both been nurtured by my unquenchable drive to live a passionate, honest life. Just like a plant stretches toward the sun, that is how I stretch. To me, it is only natural for vegans to be feminists and feminists to be vegans. Otherwise, it seems that something went wrong with the growth of the seed somewhere.

WHEN VEGANS (ALMOST) RULE THE WORLD

The food animals most abused and exploited are female. The layer hens that produce egg after egg until they are calcium deficient, crippled and spent at a year or so. The female dairy cows with swollen, infected udders and prolapsed uteruses, having been turned into virtual meat and milk machines. The enslavement in cages and crowded buildings, the forced impregnations (rape in our species), the stealing of babies, of milk intended for their babies. To my mind, it is only natural for a feminist to be deeply and personally appalled. And thus it seems natural to me that feminists should strive toward a vegan diet. (I do understand that this is part of the luxury of my privilege talking: just the fact that I can choose what to eat and what not to eat is a position of enormous privilege.)

By the same token, it would seem that a vegan - someone who is guided by principles of compassion and freedom and the inherent dignity of all - would be a feminist. As has been documented frequently in our shock-value driven popular culture, this is not a natural conclusion for all. I have been disappointed and perplexed again and again by those I assume I am walking shoulder-to-shoulder with, only to discover that my vegan colleagues - people who will stand up for a newborn chick's right to autonomy and dignity - think it's perfectly acceptable for a woman to strip on camera while reciting statistics about the exploitation of animals. The refusal to acknowledge and address the obvious intersectionalities of exploitation is one of my biggest disappointments with both feminist and vegan communities. What is the hold up?

I am far from perfect. I stick my foot in my mouth, act impulsively, look at the world from a position of privilege way too often. I understand that. The point is, though, to evolve, right? To find areas that are malnourished and cultivate them better. I don't think it's enough to acknowledge weakness, shrug and say, well, that's how I am. Of course we need to accept that we're imperfect, but striving toward ethical consistency is not the same thing as perfectionism, at least not to me. I know that we all have contradictions and areas of inconsistency: is it enough to just admit to that? I don't think so, not if we're trying to live mindfully.

I guess part of the answer is that we all have different orientations and interpretations of things. Relativism gets on my nerves, though, so much blunting of anything worth saying. Perhaps an answer is that veganism is more specific: it expects certain beliefs and practices, though anyone who has spent time with a group of vegans knows that we are hardly walking in lockstep on everything. Feminism, though, is more open to interpretation, less specific, more personal in ways. I can accept that, totally. But for vegans to downplay the importance of feminism, well, that is highly agitating to me. Same thing for feminists who choose to ignore their participation in oppression as omnivores. It seems clear that I haven't changed much from that little girl who simply did not understand disconnection: I am still seeking integration and connection everywhere and am deeply rattled when it's not there.

One day, it'll all make sense. Or I'll just learn to live with that which doesn't.

WHEN VEGANS (ALMOST) RULE THE WORLD

A Field Guide To Vegans of North America
Originally posted on Thursday, January 14, 2010

In North America, there are a small but distinct variety of vegans that have been identified frequently as the most prominent types, though some seem to cluster in certain geographic areas, and some are virtually unknown in other parts. If a vegan should be observed in the environment near your home, it is wise to have some sense of his extraction so you know his basic characteristics. Each should be approached and communicated with in a manner that is agreeable to his particular subset. Please note that as the vegans migrate into new environments, novel varieties are born. For example, some vegan-watchers claim to have had fleeting encounters with an entirely new genus best described as Conservative Republican vegans, though no photographic evidence exists yet. Another emerging subset is the Breeder vegans, feeding and nurturing their fledgling young as the next generation of vegans.

Thus far, the following vegan subsets have been confirmed as existing genera:

We have the **Groovy Latter Day Hippie Vegans (Groovy V's)** who spread good vibes (and some may say body odor) wherever they go.

We have the **Angry Young Vegans (Angry Young V's)** who want to smash the state and the stupid bourgeoisie.

We have the **Middle-Aged to Elderly Ladies (Cat Lady V's)** with the surfeit of feline companion animals and almost certainly unhygienic home.

We have the **Raw Foodists (Raw Foodie V's)** who judge others by their intestinal flora are noted for their extreme consumption of enzymes.

We have the **Politically Correct Vegans (P.C. V's)** who are primarily motivated by gaining feminist, progressive and anti-corporate credentials.

We have the **Hot Young Vegans (Hot Young V's)** who take off their clothes to make some sort of statement or whatever about cruelty to animals.

We have the **Lonely, Isolated Vegans (Lonely V's)** who live solitary lives and are the only ones many know and thus are always on display.

Groovy V's

Almost all have been born after the original hippie's flourishing period of the 1960s but they often mimic their predecessors with a pitch-perfect accuracy. They are the most colorful of the various varieties of vegans.

Diet: Groovy V's love solar power-cooked burritos, sunflower seeds, hemp seeds and they horde carob for special occasions. They prefer to gather food in bulk.

Natural habitat: The entire Pacific Northwest, Northern California, the Rainbow Gathering, the Phish show, assorted college towns, or at the dustiest co-op in town.

Nest: A VW bus re-jiggered to run on bio-fuel, a treehouse, a best friend's couch, or a cooperative living arrangement.

Migration: Planning to go to Costa Rica where they will start a B & B or begin a biodynamic farm when they get enough cash together.

Males: Long hair, gauzy clothing, tie-dyes, grooming not a priority, dilated pupils.

Females: Identical to males.

Mating rituals: Home-brewed kombucha, patchouli-scented soap and bootlegged recordings of the Dead show in '87 are used as tools of seduction.

Angry Young V's

Angry Young V's are usually only spotted in their teens or twenties. They are known for their likelihood to be clad head-to-toe in black, serious mien and general loathing and distrust of anyone who is not of their genus, therefore anyone who is not an Angry Young V should approach them with caution Interestingly, at some point unique to each (but approximately around the age of 28), they usually age out of Angry Young V identifiers and transform themselves into a different variety or out altogether.

Diet: Whatever is cheapest at the local vegetarian café, peanut butter and jelly sandwiches, Tings and chips and salsa. Also, whatever vegan food they can gather together from their mother's refrigerator or assorted favored dumpsters.

Natural habitat: Straight edge shows, the used CD store, rehearsing in a garage, the local skate park, typing angrily wherever computer keyboards can be found.

Nest: Generally resides in an apartment in a city or a college town above a Mexican restaurant, their parent's house or mate's nest.

Migration: Planning to get to New York ASAP.

Males: Spiky crest, covered in colorful, artificial markings upon his skin.

Females: Plumage is often an unnatural pigment, and, like males, her flesh is usually distinguished by its colorful markings.

Mating rituals: Seeing a show together, working on a 'zine, going to an anti-fur protest, then drinking coffee together until 3:00 a.m.

Cat Lady V's

Every town has one. She is always thinking about her cats, talking about her cats, worrying about her cats and separating squabbling cats. She carries photos of them in her wallet and has created a special song for each one of her cats. Note: there is a Dog Lady V equivalent of the Cat Lady V but she adapts and camouflages herself better to mainstream society. The Cat Lady V is quite happy with her solitary-but-for-cats existence or in the occasional company of others of her genus.

Diet: She doesn't need to eat, she'll just graze. Feeding Mr. FooFoo, TeeTee, Lulu and Miss MooMoo is the priority. Whatever the Cat Lady V does eat is dusted liberally with cat fur but she doesn't mind.

Natural habitat: She does not like to leave her nest.

Nest: Do not ever show up at her home unannounced. You must give her at least a week's notice and she's not going to be happy about it even then. She usually has her own house that she's lived in for forty years and she's not going anywhere.

Migration: She has no desire to ever migrate so you will only find her at her nest or out buying cat food and kitty litter. The only known migration pattern for the Cat Lady V is from her house to the senior citizen home.

Males: No known males exist of this variety.

Females: With hastily penciled on eyebrows when out of their nest and often scented like kitty litter, the Cat Lady V's are usually unconcerned about grooming.

Mating rituals: None observed.

Raw Foodie V's

Raw Foodie V's can be found throughout the country but are primarily found in warm climates as they love their year-round growing seasons. They have been known to break into the Proud Warrior yoga pose without warning and they are utterly devoted in their pursuit of consuming maximum enzymes. Often confused with or even interchangeable with Groovy V's, the Raw Foodie V views any personal physical imperfection - whether it's a pimple or a cold - as a healing crisis. As much as they love to interact with other varieties of vegans and other species, they are usually shunned.

Diet: Superfoods, cacao, medjool dates, acai, kale, chia seeds, sprouts, young coconuts, coconut milk, walnuts, almonds, mangos, goji berries, carrot juice.

Natural habitat: the produce section of the natural foods store, their gardens, the monthly raw potluck, foraging, prone on a table getting acupuncture or a colonic, yoga class. These are very active birds!

Nest: Apartments filled with wheat grass, dehydrators, blenders, juicers and sprouting trays in Southern California, Florida or Hawaii. If not there, they are on their way there as soon as their lease is up.

Migration: See above.

Males: Slender, bright eyed, eager demeanor.

Females: Same as males.

Mating rituals: After Hot Yoga sessions, Raw Foodie V's attempt to seduce by reducing their talk about enzymes and their intestinal state.

P.C. V's

Just the merest glimpse of a P.C. V in nature has the power to make you question all your decisions, from where you buy your clothes to how your coffee was grown to how well you've been maintaining gender neutrality in your life. P.C. V's have a very serious demeanor, second only to the Angry Young V's, perhaps fed in part by their steady diet of too many soul-crushing documentaries. Despite this, they are matched only by Raw Foodie V's as the biggest vocalizers of the subsets and they can often be seen posturing when in close proximity to other P.C. V's, which is known to bring out aggressive tendencies in the breed.

Diet: Fair-trade, organic, in season and locally grown by family farmers. If their food doesn't have at least one certification sticker on it, they are disinclined to consume it.

Natural habitat: Urban areas, college campuses, libraries, with books spread out around them at the local feminist collective café.

Nest: Their dwellings are primarily characterized by the lack of natural light, which is obstructed by piles of books authored by Noam Chomsky, Naomi Klein and Gore Vidal, among others. They are the subset most at risk of developing a Vitamin D deficiency for this reason and for their general aversion to outdoor activity.

Migration: Wherever they have the best chance of getting tenure, the Bay area or Northampton, MA.

Males: Males come in two general varieties, disheveled and neat. The disheveled are usually seen wearing the same materials as the previous day, and the neat exhibits better grooming habits and is most comfortable in formal attire.

Females: Also come in disheveled and neat varieties.

Mating rituals: When the books on order at the library haven't come in yet and the new batch of documentaries and art films are still due to arrive. the P.C. V will occasionally initiate or consent to mutually gratifying sexual contact.

Hot Young V's

The most recent genus discovered, the Hot Young V's attract a lot of attention from vegan-watchers for their willingness to display their flesh whenever the occasion should arise or if it seems to suit their purposes even remotely. The Hot Young V has been photographed more than any other genus and has had her image displayed in the most variety of media: television, print, etc. Lack of attention is the greatest threat to the Hot Young V population.

Diet: Yes. Always.

Natural habitat: Naked in cages by the circus, naked by the fast food eatery, naked on "Shock Jock" radio programs, naked in their shunning of fur. The Hot Young V's reside mostly in Southern California and New York but there is an active hotspot in Norfolk, VA. If there is a group of gawking spectators, it is likely a naked or partially clothed Hot Young V has been sighted.

Nest: For a genus so rarely seen clothed, their dwellings are surprisingly filled with numerous articles of clothing.

Migration: They seek mild climates in order to best pursue their behavioral habits.

Males: Rarely seen but observed in the field. Far outnumbered by females. He can be distinguished by his male sexual organs on display or coyly obscured.

Females: Usually possess long hair, colorful markings on her lower back and can be distinguished from the males by characteristics that are consistent with the female physique.

Mating rituals: A very flirtatious genus, the Hot Young V's try to entice members of the male persuasion to respond to their display by strutting and preening while molting themselves of clothing.

Lonely V's

Lonely V's are the most isolated of the vegans, usually found in small or rural towns with the closest vegetarian restaurant being two-to-three hours away. Vegans in general tend to cluster together, but the Lonely V's are off on their own, usually due to circumstances they are suffering through until they can leave, and they are rarely in the company of others of his or any other subset. Lonely V's, however, are committed and proud members of their species, even if they are so frequently misunderstood.

Diet: Largely they reproduce recipes off the internet they adapt to the ingredients available for them to gather.

Natural habitat: Lonely V's can be found in small towns throughout the country. They will occasionally eat at the Chinese restaurant in closest proximity to their homes but don't eat out much beyond that, They can also be seen poking forlornly through the produce section of their own grocery store. They cheer up considerably during farmer's market seasons. They also spend much of their day communicating with other vegans on computers.

Nest: They mostly reside in dwellings filled with the most recent vegetarian publications and magazine issues. Many are teenagers still living with their parents, or they are adults, married to non-vegans.

Migration: They will move as soon as they can, they assure everyone who will listen. They have been known to journey as many as four-hours from their nest for the closest vegan meet-up.

Males: Displays characteristics consistent with depressed body language.

Females: Same as males.

Mating rituals: They shower prospective mates with educational materials in the form of brochures, books and DVDs and cook extravagant vegan meals.

This list, of course, is incomplete. As noted earlier, emergent and pre-emergent genera have been observed. Please let us know any other varieties to add to subsequent editions.

Thank you!

WHEN VEGANS (ALMOST) RULE THE WORLD

Random Things That Only Other Vegans Will Be Able to Innately Understand

Originally posted on Friday, May 3, 2013

Did you know that vegans possess: Superior knowledge? Uncanny intuitive abilities? A new emotional spectrum? The ability to perform feats of uncommon cunning? Being a vegan in this world is a little like being a circus performer in that we have quirky little idiosyncrasies that are uniquely ours, though ours are adapted by swimming against the current in our culture. Some traits are impressive and useful, others are simply bizarre and perhaps annoying, but all of them are interesting.

As a vegan, you alone understand...

• The concern that you may actually be creating a new lung disease from inhaling too much nutritional yeast.

• That feeling of being super-excited when someone tells you that she is thinking about giving up meat but you feel like you have to sit on your hands to not start jumping around in excitement so instead, you pretend to be all blasé while you're mentally checking off every link you are going to send her.

• When you go to your first all-vegan event and you know that you can eat anything there but you still can't stop asking if everything is vegan because you are so used to having to do that. Oh, and then you end up eating every speck of food you can get your hands on just because it's vegan.

• You sometimes want to tell the rest of the world that vegans totally knew kale before everyone else did.

• You are the one who your co-worker goes to when her cousin wants to ask some questions because her ex-tennis partner is considering going vegan but is worried because she heard soy will kill her.

• You learn about a new vegan cheese that's just The Best! and you're all "Z!O!M!G!how-can-i-get-some?!" and you spend all day trying to track some down unsuccessfully but it's all forgotten when you hear about the new vegan Butterfingers-style candy bar and then you spend another day in fruitless pursuit of that instead. You console yourself knowing that tomorrow there will be something else you can't get until the novelty has worn off.

- When your best friend breaks up with the "last hetero vegan male on earth," you listen to a Colleen Patrick-Goudreau podcast together over a box of tissues and some Fair-Trade chocolates before helping her create a new profile on a vegan dating site.

- The anxiety you feel when dining out with a group of meat-eaters and the idea to order "family style" is brought up.

- You have a habit of scoping out someone else's animal product-free grocery cart ("cart snooping") when you're in the checkout line and then trying to figure out a non-creepy icebreaker to find out if he's vegan. You're not even sure why you need to know this.

- You can skim a label, a menu and a recipe like you've graduated magna cum laude from the Evelyn Wood Reading Dynamics program. Relatedly, you can look at any recipe and see within moments how easily you can modify it to being vegan.

- Upon hearing that a celebrity is vegan, you're all like, "Yeah, right. Not falling for that one again. Next!"

- The first thing you look at with a pair of shoes you like is not the price but the manufacturer's tag inside it. (I don't have to explain this because the vegans will understand.)

- You align yourself with the Abolitionists and you are not even a Civil War reenactor.

- The server at your local Thai place automatically repeats back to you, "Tofu, no fish sauce, no eggs," before you even order.

WHEN VEGANS (ALMOST) RULE THE WORLD

• You consciously route out your trip through the grocery store so you won't have to pass the corpses.

• If you are a freelance writer, you refer to animals as "he" and "she" and this is duly noted by your editor but whatever. She can take out your pronouns but you won't.

• The first thing you look at when you visit another vegan's home is her cookbook collection, which might even be more impressive than your own, you note with awe.

• Your egg salad sandwich that supposedly tastes "JUST like eggs!" probably won't to omnivores but that's perfectly okay. (Similarly, when we say, "You can't taste the difference," about anything we make, well, that's probably not true but, again, perfectly okay.)

• You understand that if you arrive at the vegan potluck even ten minutes after people start eating, all that will be left for you to eat are some oily craisins at the bottom of a bowl so you always arrive early to, um, help set up.

• When you see children eating red popsicles and you know that in addition to the high fructose corn syrup, they are eating tiny cochineal insects.

• You possess an encyclopedic knowledge of every way in which humans abuse other animals.

• You understand that building excitement as you are reading the ingredients on a label but then the crushing disappointment when you are 3/4 of the way through reading it and you see the words "whey" or "lanolin."

• You bring your own food when you visit your parents, even if you're only there for a couple of hours. You also find yourself in the rare role reversal of admonishing your parents to eat their vegetables.

• When the only item a restaurant offers is a hummus wrap, it feels like an act of aggression against your very person.

• When you and your vegan friends talk about someone you know who is an ex-vegan, your somber, hushed tones makes it sound like you're talking about somebody who has died in a horrible accident. Conversely, it may sound like the person is an axe murderer.

• You automatically can name a couple of vegan restaurants in practically every major (as well as some minor) U.S. city whether you've been there not. You may even be very familiar with the menu, weekly specials, and Yelp rating.

All this and more...

WHEN VEGANS (ALMOST) RULE THE WORLD

The Case for Why Vegan Feminists Should Just Rule the World Already

Originally posted on Wednesday, March 16, 2011

Do I really need to count the reasons why? Yes. Yes, I do.

A real live vegan feminist is the best kind of person to know. This is not opinion: this is scientifically provable fact. She has the most interesting array of friends, knows the best restaurants, books, films and music, and she will make you laugh and laugh with her impressions of stupid, annoying people. The vegan feminist will bring more cultural savvy and belly laughs into your life. Trust this.

While the rest of the world is tittering over the latest antics of a celebrity who is having a public nervous breakdown or psychotic episode, vegan feminists are too busy actively cultivating a whole different reality to notice or care. That's how cool and above it all we are.

We organize vegan bake sales that raise thousands of dollars to make the world a better place in our spare time, and, no, there's not a lot of time to spare what with these misogynist wing-nuts running around everywhere ruining everything. Still, we manage.

We are equally nimble at discussing the intersectionalities of oppression or this really great recipe we found for dairy-free Eggplant Parmesan. Some of us have also been known to talk about the really awesome shoes we found online.

Now that peak oil has come and gone, vegan feminists on bikes will be the incandescent symbol of the new world order. It's inevitable: we will be the next icons. What? It's not going to be a violently apoplectic tea partier with a stupid haircut, I guarantee it. Best to befriend a vegan feminist now rather than seem like a johnny-come-lately.

Despite our reputation of being a bunch of sanctimonious scolds, we have a great sense of humor, because, really, how could you live in this world and not have one? We can even laugh at ourselves. For example, how many vegan feminists does it take to screw in a light bulb? Answer: THAT'S NOT FUNNY.

With possible food shortages looming, vegan feminists are powerful allies. We cannot only make a great dinner out of just basmati rice, kalamata olives, vegetable scraps and a can of coconut milk, and we can organize a kick-ass potluck in our sleep.

We don't sleep, by the way. Too much to do. Like brainstorm meals and organize potlucks.

When life gives us lemons, we make organic, Fair Trade lemonade and we grate the rind for later use so as to not be wasteful, then we sell the lemonade to help support an awesome cause. Why? What do you do with lemons?

Some of us have children, some of us would rather adopt a pack of asocial, peri-menopausal jackals. Some of us wear make up, some consider lip balm an obvious doorway to selling out the sisterhood. Vegan feminists of today like to keep you guessing. In other words, we're not all wearing hemp power suits and swaying to the dulcet harmonies of the Indigo Girls on our iPods. In other other words, watch what you say.

Looking for a book recommendation? Fiction [Science fiction? Dystopian? Fantasy? Young Adult? Post-modern?] ? Non-fiction? Biography? Memoir? We'll send you our lists. Is it okay if they're not alphabetized?

Who's going to help you move? Who's going to pick you up from the airport? Who's willing to sniff the questionable Vegenaise? Well, it might not always be a vegan feminist, but if we say that we will do it, we'll do it. Why? Because we are dedicated friends who keep our word and because we are fearless.

Vegan feminists will listen to you complain about your life with sensitivity and understanding but hold you to a high standard of changing the things you can. Because we believe in you, that's why, and because we don't coddle.

When a local newscaster smugly narrates forage of a woman stripping to save the polar bears or minks or whatever, do not blame the vegan feminists for the bad press. Nobody consulted us on this.

Who's starting wars? Who's undermining unions? Who's hunting deer and whales? Who's letting their dogs poop everywhere and not cleaning up after them? Who's generally screwing things up miserably? Not vegan feminists.

At the end of the day, or even the beginning, we rock because we're funny, critically engaged, whip-smart, fierce, compassionate and consistent. Vegan feminists are hard at work trying to make the world suck a little less: what other subculture could say the same thing and be able to actually, you know, point to proof of it?

If vegan feminists ruled the world, there would be beautiful gardens everywhere, Rush, Glenn, and Sarah would be the names of our poodle mixes, and chocolate would be a birthright (it's all organic, Fair Trade and dark because we rule so we can just call it chocolate now). We'd have to dedicate no time to cleaning up messes caused by stupid, sexist, right-wing windbags and selfish corporate opportunists. What does this mean? More time for creative self-expression, bike rides and potlucks. This is why vegan feminists should just rule the day already.

Who's with me?

Omnivore: Fail

Originally posted on Wednesday, November 24, 2010

This essay was born of the recent trend of people publicly disavowing their once passionately held vegan or vegetarian beliefs. For many years, when people would identify themselves to me as former vegetarians, I would counter, tongue-in-cheek, that I was a former omnivore. This is my attempt to flesh out my inability to thrive - emotionally, spiritually and physically - as an omnivore.

I wanted to be an omnivore. I really did.

The path from which I began straying from omnivorism was painful, difficult, heart-wrenching even. People might try to tell me that I did something wrong, that I just didn't try hard enough, but they are mistaken: I tried with all my being to live as an omnivore. When it shattered around me, I wondered how could something that I believed with such a passionate, deeply held conviction - that animals were ours to do what we pleased with - be wrong? Who was I if I were no longer an omnivore? My core values, my deepest beliefs about my place on the earth, were inextricably tied to my omnivorism. When things started going downhill with my animal consumption, when it no longer felt like a natural or decent thing to do, I grieved for that part of myself that I was losing and desperately tried to cling to it more tightly. It was no use, though: eating animals was making me sick, literally and figuratively. Toward the end, it was clear that I was just going through the motions.

If I can trace my falling out with omnivorism, the path would lead back to our family dog. His being helped to usher in the first inkling that something was wrong. I could observe that he had emotions, that he had preferences and the same reasons anyone else would have for not wanting to be exploited, abused, killed.

33

WHEN VEGANS (ALMOST) RULE THE WORLD

Then, somehow, this view expanded outward, try as I might to contain it, and it grew like a thing out of control to encompass the birds, pigs, cows. Before I knew it, it no longer felt justifiable or rational to eat some but not others.

In other words, it no longer felt natural.

That first bite of cheeseless pizza was something I dreaded but in reality, it was remarkably easy and welcoming. Despite this new consciousness that nagged at me, I tried to continue to live like I had grown accustomed to living, to put cheese on that pizza. I even tried to put chicken on it, but I couldn't bring myself to live the lie any longer. When I threw away the cheese, tossed the chicken in the garbage, it just felt so profoundly right: even more, when I piled the pizza high with gorgeous roasted vegetables, a cornucopia from our local farms, it just felt so correct, deep inside, and I felt the ancient echo of uncomplicated contentment I had been missing from my life for so long as an omnivore. I don't know if I had ever been so hungry or had that innate hunger so completely satisified. Yes, my starving soul nearly screamed with each voluptuous bite of silky roasted vegetables and chewy crust, yes.

I knew then that my days as an omnivore were numbered. I was entering a territory I'd long scorned and derided. The more I tried to force my body to listen to my head, the more it became an inevitability: my body was insisting on becoming herbivorous despite my most fervent wishes.

Nearly from the beginning, when I would see produce in the farmers markets, I realized that there was no escaping the fact that I was part of their demise. The snow peas, proud carrots, pears, ripe little raspberries: they once burst with life. In the market, they are still colorful and plump, but they are no longer alive. They were killed for me. Not long after dabbling in veganism, I realized that I couldn't ask another to do bring these plants to market without being able to face the process myself, so as I moved away from omnivorism, I decided to start my own garden. At first, I started small, just a few packets of salad greens in a sunny little patch, but as I've fully moved toward a life rich in plant material, it has since grown much larger.

As uncertain as I was at first, I still took deep pride in the tender shoots that confidently sprang up and thrived because of my care, because of my nurturing. They could be natural, fully realized vegetables in their ideal setting with the sun warming their leaves, the wind in blowing through their stems, rain gulped thirstily by their roots. That first year of gardening, I understood on a deeper level something that I'd always known: to live was also to die, and that the natural order after birth and life would be death. When it came time to pluck those first spring lettuces, soft, sweet and delicate like a baby's satiny cheek, I was distraught. I cried and thought of asking a friend to do it instead, one who had done this many times before in his own garden. "No," I told myself. "No, I need to do this."

And so I took a deep breath and I did it, tentatively at first. My stomach hurt, my hands seemed shaky. The peppery arugula, the red leaf, the baby mizuna, they yielded at once to my touch, like a sigh. They were so alive at one moment, so clearly no longer attached to the earth the next. As much as it pained me to admit it, pulling them just felt natural and right. The depth to which I felt that I was at the right place at the right time doing the right thing was profoundly stirring. Once the initial sadness subsided, I immediately realized that I was doing more than pulling up plants. I was reconnecting with my vegetable-loving ancestors. My fingers were digging in the rich soil, pulling up the plants and brushing off the dirt to return to the cycle of life and death in my garden. It felt like a dance. The thing I thought I would never do - could never do - felt as intuitive and native to me as anything I'd ever experienced. And I thanked the greens as I collected them in my colander: thank you for giving your life to me.

Almost immediately after I quietly shifted from being an omnivore, I found that I had more energy. I felt lighter, liberated, and the heaviness I'd once felt after a big meal filled with meat and cheese was no longer evident. My heart was light, too, unburdened of the weight of all those hard, undigestible feelings that I'd suppressed for so long. I felt like singing to the world, "This feels right! Finally, I am back to being who I was meant to be!"

I dared not tell my friends, though, the omnivores who expected me to maintain the status quo, who expected me to eat chicken wings with them, to laugh at the selfish, smug meat-abstainers we knew. How could I keep my secret safe at Super Bowl parties, after-work get-togethers, holiday meals? The thought of my parents and how they would accept this betrayal of them and the core omnivorous values they raised me with brought me the most pain and worry. It was too much to bear at times and I suffered in my silence. I continued to eat my delicious stir-fries and curries, but I did it alone, surreptitiously, the light from the refrigerator the only thing illuminating me in my quiet, now-herbivorous kitchen.

Eventually, I couldn't keep up the charade any longer and the deception I'd created came crashing around me. How many times could I tell co-workers that, no, I was saving money so I would not be going to order with them from the chicken place before they'd realize that something was up? How many creative ways could I conceal the lack of meat in my lunch before people begin to notice? How many times could I fail to take antacids or suffer from heartburn before those around me would start to wonder? When it all crashed down around me, precipitated by a busybody and a vegan cookbook I'd carelessly left out on my desk, it was horrifying but it was also a relief. The double-life I'd be leading was shattered, a permanent fissure finally ripped through. I could no longer keep the lie alive.

So today in the spirit of full disclosure, I lay myself bare. I am a failed omnivore. I did my best, I really did, for years and years but it just didn't work. The hamburgers, chicken wings, tuna casserole...ew. It's not you, it's me. Instead, when I bite into roasted red peppers, grilled corn on the cob, mangoes, black bean burgers, guacamole, I know this is me as I am. It just feels right. I love the voluptuousness, the harmlessness, the juicy, life-sustaining properties and I am no longer going to be shamed into hiding.

I am a failed omnivore. Judge me if you must, but please know that I tried my very best.

WHEN VEGANS (ALMOST) RULE THE WORLD

All Beings Tremble

Originally posted on Tuesday, November 15, 2011

"All beings tremble before violence. All fear death. All love life. See yourself in others. Then whom can you hurt? What harm can you do?" – Buddha

Sometimes it just feels like being there can knock my legs out from under me.

Whenever I go to an animal sanctuary, I become acutely aware of my personal failings. It seems like an incongruous thing, feeling so peaceful with the rescued animals and pastoral setting but not being able to ignore the particular flaws that have come into high relief. This awareness doesn't prevent me from enjoying myself, just sort of buzzes underneath the surface, a mosquito of little consequence but still an irritant.

I don't usually think of myself as an especially resentful person, but the animals and their willingness to trust people after all we have done to them are a reminder that I still have a lot of work to do. Whenever I go to an animal sanctuary, I am reminded that forgiveness is a deeply challenging practice for me, as though if I have resentment against those who have hurt me in the past, it will transcend the time-space continuum and stick to them like a barnacle. The animals don't hold on to anything and they have seen and survived far worse than I. I remember this also from when I worked at an animal shelter: dogs who had been starved to near-skeletal conditions, cats who had been used as bait in pitbull fights, beings that had known little to no human kindness, still ran up to the cage door, eager to greet us. I will never forget the cat I met at the shelter, very disfigured from having been set on fire, rubbing his raw skin against the cage bars, purring at the sight of me, a stranger. A human. We can be terrible co-inhabitants on this home we share but they don't seem to resent us.

Last June, as I do every summer, I spent the day with my family and friends at SASHA Farm, a Michigan refuge for animals primarily from the agriculture industry, where the residents rush to the fences to greet us. Yes, we had strawberries and apples and carrots, but even when we had run out, they stretched out toward us, seeking a hand, a friendly face. They looked at us without guile. The cows, with their wet, innocent eyes, always impress me with their gentleness. The goats, lively and rambunctious, climb over one another to grab carrots, they bleat with confidence and conviction. The tom turkeys strut with their feathers spread out like intricate fans, almost begging to be admired; the chickens look at us with unabashed, courageous curiosity, especially counter to their public reputation. It's as if the animals know that they are safe now, these beings who almost all suffered horrific abuse, who were forcibly removed from their mothers and siblings as newborns. It's more than that, though: it's as if the horrors they lived through never happened.

You can still see it on them, though, like marker transparencies lain over their three-dimensional forms. Hens with bumpy, pink patches of skin where feathers should be, that's one indication. A goat with a circle cut through his ear like he'd been through a hole-puncher. He had. The cow with little white nubs where her horns were once, lasting evidence of the systematic, everyday brutality she endured. Pigs inflated to such an enormous size to satisfy the demand for their flesh that they could barely move.

The routine deformities we can see in the survivors of animal agriculture is often the most obvious display of the cruelty they endure in the process of being turned from a living animal into a product to be consumed and forgotten. In the ultimate objectification, the animals are turned into mere vehicles for their own consumable flesh and what their bodies produce, the things we say we "can't live without." Engineered for their flesh, so-called broiler hens are conceived with a natural expiration date: our tour guide at SASHA explained that these birds don't live past the age of one. They die of congestive heart failure before that, victims of our preference for their plump breasts, our meat. On this day, though, and on all the days since they found sanctuary at SASHA, the chickens scratched at the dirt, felt the sun on their wings, they lived as natural, fully realized beings. The expiration date ticks but they enjoy life. We ravaged their bodies but their spirits, if given half a chance, are unsinkable.

There is so much that we take for granted and the power we humans wield – not necessarily in strength but in the privileges we aim to protect - overwhelms me when I think about it. We can ruin someone else's perfectly nice day simply because we feel like it, or we can ruin another's life because we don't want to question the liberties we'd prefer to keep enjoying. Sometimes it doesn't take much to make me angry: A spilled glass of water, a misplaced set of keys, a train that I missed by five seconds. The anger I can feel over these trivial hardships frightens me. Once in a while, too, I lose my temper with my son. Imagine how that lopsided power structure feels to someone half your size to experience: a raised voice, a mean look, even a clenched hand from someone who could inflict real damage. My potential to harm my child, the one I most want to protect in the world, the soul who most fills me with joy, is a terrifying thing to own and I live my life with the knowledge of it. I have never hit my son and I never expect to intentionally harm him. We exist with an inherent power imbalance that dramatically skews in our favor, though, as adult humans. We cannot do whatever we want to simply because we have the privileges, preferences and opportunities: we should have learned as young children that this is not a moral way to operate.

All beings want to live without imprisonment and cruelty: if we are honest, we will admit that humans are not unique in this regard. We will also admit that all beings want the same for their babies. As consuming others as products is both unnecessary and necessitates violence, then it is an indulgence and there is a moral imperative to withdraw our support from it.

All beings tremble before violence.

Of course we do.

All fear death.

This only makes sense.

All love life.

All beings crave the things that make us feel good: warm sun, affection, the pure, visceral joy that shoots through us on that first beautiful spring day. To deny this is arrogance.

See yourself in others.

If you do, it will be hard to maintain your privileges.

Then whom can you hurt?

What harm can you do?

WHEN VEGANS (ALMOST) RULE THE WORLD

On My Indoctrinated Vegan Child
Originally posted on Wednesday, February 15, 2012

Not too long ago, my son made quite a debut online. He was actually "trending" around the holidays. A video project that we created for his class to demystify veganism grew into something much larger when my husband posted it on YouTube <http://youtu.be/WdXbwFO3LT8> and I shared it on Facebook. I knew that a few of my friends would have a good kvell but had no idea that it would take on a life of its own. Who would guess that there would be a large number of people interested in hearing a nine-year-old talk about his life as a vegan? Through the sudden intimacy the Internet forges, my son's simple, heartfelt message managed to spread far beyond his classroom, and I found myself encouraging isolated parents raising young vegans in rural towns in the South, getting support from amazing activists in Madrid, reading messages filled with so much love - yes, love - and enthusiasm from all over the world. All because of a video we didn't even think to make our son brush his hair for (and we won't make that mistake again).

We let that wave of good cheer wash over us even while I was looking over my shoulder in expectation of the ripple of bitterness swelling up behind us and, indeed, when it arrived, it threatened to knock my legs out from under me. A popular website with a lot of followers picked up and posted my son's video and within a minute or two, the inflammatory comments started rolling in.

Never mind that my son didn't even speak negatively about eating animals or meat-eaters: he simply talked about his life. For that matter, people who eat animals were not addressed at all in his video. I have learned that there is little that can get under the skin of privileged people more than to make them feel that they are not at the center of attention. He was simply talking about his life and that managed to be threatening and offensive to people. This didn't surprise me too much because I remember this phenomenon from my years of hanging out with feminist activists: I found it fascinating that the women who were not interested in men in the slightest – not to be attractive to or sleep with - got far more of a rattled, defensive reaction than those who were openly critical. I can only think that this indifference threatens the foundational privilege of being the center of everything more. This is another exploration for another day, though.

What I was most taken aback by, though, was the charge leveled against us of indoctrination. I'd heard that hinted at before ("But aren't you going to let him decide for himself if he's going to eat meat?") but there is something about that first experience of having a bunch of strangers pitch insults against you as a parent and as a person that makes it much more viscerally felt. We were dangerous and extreme. We were irresponsible and using our son to advance our agenda. We were indoctrinating an innocent child.

Let's consider the word "indoctrinate." One could successfully argue that veganism promotes a particular worldview and certain values. It is undeniable that my husband and I embrace the core values central to veganism – constructing our lives so that we operate from our convictions about compassionate living – as central in our son's development and education. There are very few examples of groups of people who tailor their lives so as to be harmonious with their values.

Wait a minute, though.

Every time someone opts to go to a McDonald's Playland with her children, this is a form of supporting one's values with her actions, isn't it? In this case, the values might be a desire for familiarity, speed, convenience and affordability. Those are not necessarily values based on convictions but they are still values of a different sort. When people pack turkey sandwiches for their children, give them string cheese and chocolate milk, doesn't this also communicate values and possibly indoctrination? Don't the scrambled eggs and bacon also send an implicit message? This is food. This is what we eat. This is okay. People are being naïve

43

or dishonest if they don't acknowledge that there is a message with that, and that even if the message is unspoken, it is still thoroughly relayed.

Yes, my son is being raised with particular values. I never have pretended otherwise. Does this mean that he is brainwashed? Hardly. We are raising him to ask questions, to not be afraid to think deeper, to think critically about our privileges and the status quo. As a child, was I educated about the food we ate? Was I given an alternative? No. We are a vegan family because these are our values as parents and anyone who thinks that the mere act of raising a child around certain values is indoctrination is not considering what all parents are supposed to do. Whether we do it actively – through discussion, exploration, and learning – or passively – through communicating our beliefs by our actions – all parents are almost certainly raising our children with certain core values. My husband and I are very mindful of this responsibility.

As opposed to someone who is indoctrinated, I would say that my son's eyes are wide open. He knows that chicken nuggets were living beings at one point. He visits chickens in person at the sanctuary we go to every year; he knows where nuggets originate. When his friends are eating cheese and sausage pizza in the cafeteria, he understands that the milk and sausage come from animals. He is under no illusions about this. He knows that hamburgers are parts of cows ground up together: is he under illusions about this? Further, he is able to use this understanding about how products are sold to us as "normal" and "natural" and apply it to other aspects of consumerism. Instead of being an instrument of indoctrination, I'd say that veganism is giving our son a point-of-entry for critical thinking.

Most children love animals. To eat them, most children are misled, misinformed or stifled as they develop and questions emerge. Wouldn't raising a child as an omnivore then create more of a fertile ground for indoctrination? There are many pernicious forms brainwashing can take. Some people don't think twice about letting corporations do it. Others trade critical thinking and compassionate living in favor of entrenched privileges, habits and traditions. Raising a child without illusions about or indifference to others' exploitation and misery is not indoctrination, though. Let's be clear on that.

It is raising a child with values.

WHEN VEGANS (ALMOST) RULE THE WORLD

My Canine Teeth and Superior Intelligence Will Help Me To Annihilate You, Rabbit

Originally posted on Tuesday, January 29, 2013

I see you, bunny.

I am a human so that means that my keen eyesight and sharp reasoning skills have helped me to deduce that you are indeed loose in my back yard.

Oh, you are going to wish that you were never born. I am salivating down my canine teeth at the thought of your tender organs in my fearsome mouth. As soon as I'm done checking my messages, I am so vanquishing you, my tender quarry.

Now I am hiding in the hydrangea bushes next to my deck, the smartest place to remain undetected, just as I would in the African savannah. The hose is coiled next to me like the most threatening python that ever lived, the rake lying there like an antelope skeleton. It's like Animal Planet back here. Stealthily, I am watching you between the branches with my laser-sharp focus. You have no idea. Crouched, I breathe silently, purposefully, and reserve my energy for that precise moment when you – Oh, damn it! My phone is vibrating in my shirt pocket. Or is that my chest, buzzing with adrenaline? Nah, it was my phone. Hair cut at 4:30.

Keep munching on that dandelion, you simple-minded little herbivore. It will be your last one. While you are doing that, I am mentally devising the best strategy for your swift but brutal end, rabbit. With cat-like grace, I will pounce, dive and grasp you in my devastating grip right before I sink my teeth in your jugular. Your resistance will be brief but noble as you find yourself in a life-or-death battle with an adversary who far outmatches you. Even your adorable little brain will grasp the futility of your struggle as you finally submit to my might and far superior mental capacity. Your end will be well-earned and so sweet. I will browse from my collection of Epicurious recipes before I finally determine the one worthy of serving as your final act. Perhaps you, some raw, small-batch goat cheese and grilled endive on that Mid-Century Modern platter I fought to the death for in a bidding war on eBay with cilantro and red bell pepper for color? A composed salad? BOOM: Pinterest that shit. If I'm not asked to be admin of the Paleo Facebook group after this, I don't know what I'm going to have to do.

I'm going to hunt-and-gather the ever-loving crap out of you, rabbit. Is it just me or is it so fucking Pleistocene back here? Oh wait, I just remembered that UPS was supposed to deliver my new GPS this afternoon. I hope he just leaves it on my stoop. But then what if someone steals it? I don't want to have to drive to Saturday's Caveman Diet Meet-Up without my GPS. Damn it. I'd better check the UPS truck location. What? No goddamn signal? Again? What is wrong with Verizon? Dumping those stooges. Oh, I am so tweeting about this. They messed with the wrong –

Wait!

Where the hell is my rabbit? GOD. I hate my life.

Sigh. You won this round, you little bastard. Next time, I am going to GPS your ass. Oh, you are going to wish you were never born. Where the hell is my delivery?!

WHEN VEGANS (ALMOST) RULE THE WORLD

The Switch Inside

Originally posted on Friday, September 18, 2009

If you have been vegan for any significant length of time, you have undoubtedly asked yourself several vexing questions during your tenure. You may have wondered why your mother persistently mispronounces the word, nearly fifteen years later. (Or maybe that's just me.) You may have speculated over why the omnivorous world seems to view you as a priest in a confessional as they lay their souls bare about their flesh-eating ways ("It-is-not-much-it-is-just-fish-I-tried-to-do-the-vegetarian-thing-but-just-couldn't-resist-my-grandma's-brisket") seeking absolution, like you are some sort of God proxy figure. And then there is the Eternal Question, the one that has nagged at us since the word vegan was first coined by that English gentleman in 1944. It usually sounds something like this: what makes me different from my omnivorous and even vegetarian friends? Why do I tick when they tock? How can I see something so very clearly when it remains obscured to my friends, my family? Further, why do I see this when others do not and how can I get them to see it, too?

We all have friends who are so progressive in every other way but for whom the diet part of the equation does not factor in much. They eat whatever is in front of them, no or few questions asked. But then there are those who are aware of their consumption habits within the context of what they eat. They may scrupulously avoid food that is out of season or shipped too far or artificial or over-packaged or produced by horrible companies, Many even will avoid the most infamously torturous "delicacies" like veal and foie gras, but the line they will not cross is a broad one and one that is very clearly rolled out in front of them. The line is more of a wide gulf, really, and it separates the vegans (a.k.a., The Crazies) from everyone else (a.k.a, The Sane Ones). Vegans have good intentions but they take it too far, they may say or broadly hint. We are absolutists, extremists, people who wake every day with the sole purpose of wrecking everyone else's good time. My question is this: when we are trying to live our lives with integrity and a certain measure of consistency, veganism could be seen as the natural extension of a general point-of-view, an intuitive conclusion to draw when taking into consideration one's whole path and perspective, right? It would be ignoring the elephant in the room for many of us to not adopt a vegan lifestyle. It is rooted in the same desire to live compassionately and mindfully, therefore it would be radical and extreme to pretend that it wasn't natural. It entirely natural if you are trying to live compassionately, are concerned about social justice, believe in your power to effect positive change.

Knowing this further compounds the confusion I feel when those who are so clearly on a similar path as mine take an entirely divergent route right exactly here, where how we live our lives and food intersect. It is as though we were walking along together, really enjoying one another's company, compatible as peas in a pod until my feet just want keep following the path – the one that seems to be the most natural one – and my non-vegan friends take an abrupt turn and bid me adieu. "You're on your own with this one, friend. Good for you but not for me," they say as they skip off and I am left baffled once again. I can think of so many examples right off the top of my head and after almost fifteen years of wondering about this, I am no closer to understanding it. There are friends who won't purchase any new clothing because they don't want to support the brutality of the sweatshop industries. They are not vegan. There are people I know who will go on a hunger strike at the drop of a hat to draw attention to the military violence overseas. When they resume eating, they eat the product of violence. There are feminists, artists, freedom seekers, peace workers, culture jammers of all variety who actively reject the consumerist-patriarchal-military-industrial-you-name-it complex but feel no conflict with eating animals and even more who do feel that inner-tug but decide to live with it anyway.

49

WHEN VEGANS (ALMOST) RULE THE WORLD

How is it that our moral compasses are so out-of-synch on this single issue, but return to being coordinated once we leave it? I know that people disagree all the time on core issues – we all have our own path, it is part of what makes us unique, blah blah blah- however when things are lined up to point in a certain direction, and then that direction takes what seems to be a random, hairpin turn, it is only natural to look back and say, What on earth just happened there? Where did you go?

Except it's not really accurate to say that I am totally confused because I do have an idea, even if it's fuzzy and only a metaphor. I tend to think of vegans as having had their switch turned on. Imagine the switch as the mechanism that turns on a light. Either it's the kind of switch that turns on a blast of light at once (the equivalent of a mental epiphany) or it's a dimmer switch, slowly illuminating a room over time (the equivalent of a slow dawning). This light switch reveals the arbitrariness, brutality and injustice of our dominion over non-humans. Occasionally people have the light switch engaged but then decide that they no longer want to see all that it exposes, or that they still do see but it doesn't affect them the same way any longer. (They can see but have turned off the corresponding feeling switch.) For most of the vegans I know, though, I would say that once that light switch turned on – either as an epiphany or a slow dawning or somewhere in between – it is stuck on. From that point on (the point being where recognition leads to an inner- and outer-transformation) our new perspective has fundamentally altered us. The veil has been removed and we can clearly see. The challenge is in coexisting with those for whom the practice of eating animals is still shrouded, either intentionally or unintentionally, and that we are asked to suspend seeing what we do so the rest of the world can continue maintaining the status quo, which is that animal parts and products are neutral and harmless, no different than broccoli or apples or kidney beans. To us, this is being complicit in a deception we have already identified and rejected.

So this is how I've come to think about vegans, as patronizing as it may very well be to omnivores: somewhere along the line, our lights were switched on. This doesn't mean about everything, that we are above reproach in all matters. It also doesn't mean that I think omnivores are entirely in the dark, Gollum-like creatures lurking in the shadows. I don't think this, never thought that. (Okay, there was probably a period in the spring of 1995 when I did, but no longer.) Vegans are just regular people who have our lights switched on. Once the light switched on, we made changes accordingly. We can be approachable and helpful, but it is a tall order to ask us to pretend not to see what is plainly obvious to us.

How do we activate this switch in another? We can't. We can leave a trail of clues to locating that switch but the other person's hand has to be on it herself. You cannot force anyone's hand, you can just sort of coax it along.

Helping others find their light switches is our work.

Top Ten Frequently Repeated, Often Illogical and Always Convenient Myths Repeated to Vegans

Originally posted Wednesday, September 12, 2012

Revisiting my previous post, I wanted to share some of the common myths and conceits that are repeated to vegans as if they were truth. I am doing this sort of as a favor to those who repeat them because, honestly, guys, you probably don't realize the regularity with which we hear them. And when we hear them, it's all we can do sometimes to be patient and not roll our eyes. You don't want to be someone who causes excessive internal eye-rolling, right? There are many, many more myths than the ones listed here and many subsets of the ones I have, but you get the idea. We've heard it all before.

1. Vegan food is expensive.

First I have to ask: compared to what? Compared to fast food? Well, yes, compared to dollar menus of hamburgers and fries, it is more costly on the surface, but the expenses of illness and obesity more than offsets this. Time spent off of work waiting in doctor's offices, scanning drugstore shelves for anti-constipation remedies, or getting arterial stents inserted is expensive.

The next question is if vegan food is truly expensive compared to meat and animal products. Quite simply, it's not.

The average price for a pound of ground beef in July of this year [2012] was $3.085. The price for a pound of dried organic black beans was $1.99 at Whole Foods. One cooks down and the other expands with cooking. The poorest people of the world are often nearly vegan by default. Let's look at what they eat: Legumes. Grains. Seasonal fruits and vegetables. Fresh herbs. Nuts and seeds. They are not eating organic, heirloom goji berries at $15.99 an ounce. They are eating simple peasant food that is grown close to home because that is the least expensive and most accessible. In our own country during the Depression, we canned and froze the harvest to make food less costly. The notion that vegan food is more expensive than animal foods is simply not fact-based. It does cost more on the surface to be discerning about what we put in our bodies but it is far more expensive down the road to be unwell. Consider eating whole, unprocessed foods another form of health insurance.

Please note that none of this is even considering the expenses our whole society takes on in cleaning up the ecological mess of animal agriculture.

2. Caring for animals prevents us from caring about people.

This is a false dichotomy born of an absolutist perspective. If one looks at the world through an either/or lens, it's a natural conclusion that advocating for some means that we cannot advocate for others. In truth, compassionate people are compassionate people. Does someone who kicks his dog have more of a reservoir of compassion for people than someone who doesn't kick his dog? We don't turn compassion on or off like a faucet and we are not born with a finite supply of it. The greater empathy you feel for others, the more empathy you will produce. It is more like a muscle than a supply. I would be far more trusting of someone's willingness to care for others who has demonstrated an ability to empathize and take courageous action on another's behalf. The people who feel we need to carefully parse our compassion? Nah. Not so much.

3. Vegans are in a cult/engage in "group-think."

Hee. This one is especially amusing to me.

Anyone who knows anything about vegans knows that you ask five of us the same question, you are likely to get five different opinions (or maybe 18 different opinions), some that may profoundly differ from one another. We will go to the mat on topics as seemingly benign as to whether we will date non-vegans and go for the jugular on the topic of what we feed our cats. The array of topics on which we will loudly disagree is truly spectacular, almost a renewable resource: whether to wear our old leather and wool items or give them away; whether or not we will eat at restaurants that serve meat; whether vegans are allowed to be motivated by health concerns over their ethical convictions; whether we support incremental animal welfare measures or most assuredly do not. This is just the tip of the iceberg. There is no shortage of topics for us to vehemently disagree with one another on and there never will be. We have no central leader, no agreed upon strategy and, honestly, no overarching goal. One thing vegans would agree upon is that we do not believe that it's our right to abuse and kill animals. From there on out, though, all bets are off.

4. We have to be 100% impeccably vegan about everything our bodies come in contact with or else we are hypocrites.

You know what? We lived in a flawed world. We live in a violent world built upon exploitative systems. Have you noticed? There is animal-derived stearic acid in car tires: even if you don't drive, it's in bike tires. Gelatin is used to make the non-digital films people see. Those beautiful vegan cookbooks? Most likely, they are held together with casein in glue. We get it.

We didn't create this mess and actually, we're the ones trying to get us out of it. The reason why there are animal-derived components in so much is because of the conceit that animals are ours to use as we wish and because, well, after eating whatever we can off of their bodies, there is a lot left over for people to make money off of still. We're trying to create a world in which we do not exploit others. We are not there yet and the world is a complicated beast with many tentacles wrapped around various forms of exploitation. We're not going to extricate ourselves overnight but at least the vegans are trying our best to minimize harm. Could you say the same?

5. Historically, there has never been a vegan culture.

Ergo? And? We are blazing trails, not creating historical reenactments.

There was never a Christian culture before Christianity. There was never a culture of feminism before pioneers created it. There was never an ecological movement until people started it. We are not limited by the past: thankfully we have self-determination. While those who are yoked to the past keep coming up with nonsensical excuses, vegans are actively creating our own burgeoning culture that can make a difference now and benefit future generations. What is more exciting and promising, having our future hemmed in by history or boldly creating one ourselves?

6. If the world went vegan, what would we do with all those animals not used for food?

This is where people really start grasping at straws.

First of all, why do you suddenly care about the tenability or sustainability of caring for billions of animals at once? Were you concerned before about the giant, leaking fecal lagoons, dead zones in the ocean, air pollution and horrific wastefulness of animal agriculture? (And, oh, bonus points for gullibility if you think that the magic wand of organic agriculture would make the giant footprint of massive animal agriculture disappear. Ta da!)

Second, who on earth said that the world would go vegan overnight? Is that at all likely? What vegans are working for at best is a world that is shifting away from animal agriculture and even the most optimistic, power-of-positive-thinking, cheerful herbivore knows that this would occur gradually. Of course. The idea that we would wake up one morning after the Vegan Revolution to chickens all over our front yards, turkeys in our trees, and cows taking over the boulevards is absurd.

What would happen to all the liberated animals if they are not born, bred and killed for our interests? Well, something tells me that we have oodles of time to figure this out. One idea: as demand eventually decreases and fewer animals are bred in order to be made into food, the populations would decrease. As populations decrease, we need less of the massive amount of land that is currently earmarked for monocropping soy, corn, and wheat that is fed to all the animals in confinement. Perhaps this land could be freed up for some of the animals to live out their lives in peace. I'm not saying that I have the answers but I am saying that we don't need them yet. Because it's not going to be overnight, that much is certain.

7. What about all the SOY?! Vegans eat too much soy and that is destroying the environment.

Okay, is it honestly logical that vegans, checking in (very optimistically) at about 2.5% of the population, are creating all this demand for soy? All those damn Boca burgers? Seriously? You know who is responsible for the monocropping of soy? Omnivores. Omnivores eat the billions of "food animals" who consume all that soy in their feed. So if you are really, truly concerned about the environmental implications of soy, it's simple. Do what I do: go vegan and limit your soy consumption. Easy peasy. And contrary to common opinion, vegans do not all eat tofu nuggets dipped in dairy-free mayo with a side of soy jerky. I buy tofu maybe twice a month. Could the omnivores say that they limit their soy consumption to this extent? (Oh, plus it's totally not an ethical argument. Do not be misled by this one.)

8. The life and death of a cow and the life and death of a tomato are roughly equivalent.

Oy vey. Science was never my topic but I will give it a shot here.

One has veins and arteries. One doesn't. One has a central nervous system. One doesn't. One has a spinal cord with nerve endings. One doesn't. One has a body designed by evolution and natural selection to avoid pain and suffering. One doesn't. One has a thalamus. One doesn't. One has a limbic system. One doesn't.

Further, one is forcibly impregnated. One isn't. One has babies who are taken from her shortly after birth. One doesn't. One calls out for them after they are taken. One doesn't. One is de-horned, branded, and castrated without anesthesia. One isn't. One has the proven capacity for emotionally bonding with her offspring and others. One hasn't. One demonstrably suffers using an empirical checklist of physical and observational yardsticks. One doesn't.

If you don't believe in evolution and your beliefs tend toward Creationism, a Great Creator, Gaia or a combination thereof, perhaps you can tell me why your compassionate creator designed beings with a proven capacity to suffer and a clear desire to avoid said suffering only to give them no possibility of escaping that pain. What was the purpose of that? Where is the intelligent design or benevolence in that? I would never believe in a creator who would be so cruel as to imbue such deeply exploited beings with sentience and emotions only to have them needlessly suffer.

One bleeds. One cries out. One writhes in pain. Making cows and tomatoes (or chickens and pears or any other animal-plant combination) peers in the capacity to feel and suffer shows how willing some omnivores are to suspend critical thinking in order to justify their habits.

9. Our bodies evolved to eat meat.

Evolution is an ongoing process. It is not static. There is plenty to contradict the notion that we are designed to eat meat (our teeth made for chewing rather than tearing, our small mouths and jaws, our lack of claws, our long, pouched long intestines) but I am not going to get into that. Evolution is, well, evolving, and thankfully we have some choice in the matter. The fact that we can live healthfully and abundantly without animal-based foods is all I need to know.

10. Native Americans showed their respect and gratitude for the meat they ate. I am doing the same.

I think that cherry-picking from various cultures in order to imbue one's habits with pseudo-spiritual values is really exploitative and self-serving. Here are some other things native cultures have done: left their sick, disabled, wounded and unwanted to die; gone hungry when food wasn't plentiful; pooped in holes in the ground. And on and on and on. How many other "Native American" habits do you maintain? Or do you just maintain the ones that make you feel that your comfortable habits are spiritual in nature rather than entitlements?

If you want to feel respect and gratitude for me, don't kill and eat me. If killing me is how you show respect and gratitude, well, then I'd rather not have it. I will just prefer sovereignty and compassion, thanks. If you have to invoke some quasi-spiritual convictions that you keep handy for justifying your habits, I'd say that this is evidence of hypocrisy and, ultimately, disrespect for the cultures you claim to respect.

What else have you got?

Soy Will Kill You DEAD

Tuesday, September 6, 2011

I am buried under work this week so I'm offering this guest post until I can dive back into vegan feminist agitating. In an effort to prove that I am as fair and balanced as they come, I'm offering this article submitted by someone who wished to remain anonymous from the Weston A. Price Foundation's Office of Soybean Literacy. I hope you enjoy it and find it enlightening.

Dear Vegans,

If you don't value your own life, please at least care about the future of others. There is a looming green menace, a bean determined to wreak havoc any place where its roots can burrow into the ground like hungry, greedy tentacles. It is dire but it's not too late: we must do our part now to uproot this vicious plant until it becomes fully indestructible and sends our planet on a collision course with obliteration. It is truly the Bad Bean. *(The following footnoted article was peer-reviewed by the board of directors of the Weston A. Price Foundation.)*

To put it bluntly, soy will kill you DEAD.[1]

Women, soy will turn your ovaries inside out before they shrink into themselves, drain down your legs and settle into your feet. This will eventually cripple you. This is a small matter because your muscles would have atrophied long before this due to Toxic Estrogenic-Legume Syndrome and your brain will have become porous with Tofu Spongiform Edamamepathy. Then you will die.[2]

Men, exposure to soy will make you grow giant breasts sloshing with soymilk. It will make your genitalia shrink into petunia-shaped little nubs[3] as the steady drip-drip-drip of phytoestrogens into your bloodstream transforms you into a grotesque quasi-female freak-form come to life. Your breasts will keep growing until they eventually smother you and endanger your community. Then you will die.[4]

Children, the soy your parents give you today will make bright pink hair sprout on your concave chests (females) and on your enormous breasts (males). At around age thirteen, boys will metamorphose into girls and girls will metamorphose into boys in a horrific live mutation. As the erstwhile girls morph into aggressive, pimply males and the former males transmute into screeching, hormone-mad girls, all ages from puberty onward are fraught with peril as you lurch into marauding delinquency. Then you will die.[5]

It is now known that soy shot Abraham Lincoln and the Archduke Ferdinand.[6] Soy insurgents caused the Spanish-American War and the Nicaraguan Civil War.[7]

Further, it is well established that soy caused the Great Chicago Fire, the San Francisco Earthquake, the Dust Bowl and the Irish Potato Famine.[8]

Soy returns movies late. Soy parks like an idiot. Soy plays horrible music too loud. Soy drunk dials. Soy leaves the faucet running. Soy never offers to pay. Soy is a sloppy drunk. Soy does not vacate its seat for the elderly or disabled on buses. Soy laughs at inappropriate times. Soy sends texts during movies. Soy eats loudly and with its mouth open. Soy relieves itself on your front yard.[9]

Soy will know just what to say. Soy will make you think that you're the only one. Soy will charm your pants off and then soy will never call again. You will run into soy on the street or at a party some time later and it will smirk at you in a way that makes you feel like dirt.[10]

It gets worse.

Soy peers into your windows at night. Soy makes you feel uncomfortable on public transit. Soy stands too close to you in the checkout lane. Soy loiters on playgrounds. Soy makes your normally confident dog whimper then run and hide in the closet. Whenever soy appears, a foreboding storm rolls in out of nowhere. Soy drives by slowly, staring at you with a menacing look that sends chills down your spine.[11]

Soy is watching you. Soy is not pleased.[12]

Soy was engineered in an underground secret government laboratory with DNA from Darth Vader, Voldemort and Freddy Krueger and then one terrible night, soy overpowered the researchers and the evening watchman and got loose, running into the pitch-black night.[13]

So please, if not for your own sake, if not for the sake of others, if not for the sake of everything decent and natural and good, please join us in this ultimate battle against the legume of death if only for the future of the planet. Once eradicated, we can celebrate over pureed organ meats, bone broth and unpasteurized milk.[14] Until that day, we must not rest! We must fight the green menace with all of our force.

Footnotes

[1] McKibble, Susan. "Soy, the Legume of Certain Painful Death" *The Journal of Soya Conspiracies* (August 2005)

[2] Keith, Frances. "Emerging Speculative Soy-Borne Diseases of the Dystopian Future," *The Daily Sun and Mail*, 1 May 2008, sec. 2, p. 17

[3] Kellis, Mark. *Penises Into Petunias: the Tofuification of Masculinity*. Self-published, 1999.

[4] O'Connor, Mary. "Population Under Threat," *The Journal of Soya Conspiracies* (June 2003)

[5] Keith, Frances. "Children: Soy's Most Innocent Casualty," *The Daily Sun and Mail*, 17 June 2004, sec. 2, p. 9

[6] Kellis, Mark. *The Secret History of the World's Most Violent Legume*. Self-published, 2001

[7] Ferdin, Josephine. "The Soybean Wars: Violence, Famine, Plagues, Disasters and the Plant that Caused Them All, Part One." *The Journal of Fringe Theories* (September 2007)

[8] Ferdin, Josephine. "The Soybean Wars: Violence, Famine, Plagues, Disasters and the Plant that Caused Them All, Part Two." *The Journal of Fringe Theories* (September 2008)

[9] Keith, Frances. "Soy, the World's Worst Neighbor," *The Daily Sun and Mail*, 15 October 2010, sec. 2, p. 11.

[10] Fawkes, Lisa. "The Misogyny of Soy: From Swaggering Tofu to Sadistic Tempeh," *The Nourishing Traditions Feminist Journal* (April 2009).

[11] Rich, Carol. "The Coming Apocalypse: Soybeans as Lucifer." *The Weston A. Price Foundation Journal of Non-Secular Thought.* (October 2010)

[12] Ferdin, Josephine. "The Soybean Wars: Violence, Famine, Plagues, Disasters and the Plant that Caused Them All, Part Three." *The Journal of Fringe Theories* (September 2009)

[13] Polonis, Toby. "The True Story of Soy: From Experiment to Modern Day Horror Story." The Journal of Fringe Theories (November 2003)

[14] O'Fairon, Fiona. Long Live Liver! *The Weston A. Price Foundation's Party Food for Nourishing Traditions.* The Weston A. Price Foundation Press, 2005

An Alphabet for Disgruntled But Ever-Hopeful Vegan Activists

Originally posted on Wednesday, December 23, 2009

This is a cynical alphabet (with little bits of hope tossed in) because sometimes it just sucks to be a vegan in an omnivorous world. You are frequently misunderstood and are often the token herbivore in mixed company. People make a sport of trying to find your inconsistencies, and if they can't find any, you are accused of being "too perfect" and self-righteous. You go to the company holiday party and once again, you've got to poke around a boiled vegetable plate and look cheerfully oblivious while the others look at you in condescending sympathy. This alphabet is for those days, when nothing seems to go right, you just got word that your all-time favorite vegan restaurant is closing, the dull-eyed guy behind the counter can't tell you what's in the three grain salad and Ringling Brothers is coming to town. You know, that sort of day.

Most of the time, you are cheerful and pleasant and welcome any challenges with the enthusiasm of a bounding Labrador, but there are days when you're just not up for it and you want to barricade yourself in your home with all your awesome vegan friends who understand you, a well-stocked kitchen and a bunch of great cookbooks. It will pass. Until it passes, though, this alphabet is for you.

A is for All the times you've been asked if you get enough protein or if your shoes are leather or if you can "just eat around it."

B is for Being patient despite wanting to scream sometimes.

C is for Carrots and Celery and Cabbage, the components of a nourishing soup that will provide the warmth you need after a long day of handing out Why Vegans.

D is for "Duh, no, my shoes aren't leather."

E is for Excellent, as in your blood pressure, at least, is excellent.

63

WHEN VEGANS (ALMOST) RULE THE WORLD

F is for Faster-than-the-speed-of-light, which is the velocity at which the best vegan comestibles disappear at the monthly potluck.

G is for Garbanzo beans because you have eaten your weight in hummus several times over.

H is for Holidays and the wool gloves your mother buys you every year that you have to exchange.

I is for Insomnia, the secret weapon of the super-productive.

J is for Jackass, something you mutter under your breath when you have just had it.

K is for Koalas, because they're darn cute and sometimes you just need to see a picture of one chewing on a eucalyptus leaf to feel better. K is also for Kucinich for pretty much the same reasons.

L is for "La la la la! I can't hear you!" which is what people may as well just come out and say sometimes.

M is for Meat Is Murder, the song that first lit a spark.

N is for "Nah-Nope-No," which is what you say when asked if you ever miss cheese, eggs or meat.

O is for "Oh my god, I can't believe I used to eat that."

P is for Pasta, the vegan's saving grace when traveling or dining out with omnivores.

Q is for Quit, which you'll never do, despite the occasional bad day.

R is for Rejoicing, which you do at the littlest victories: When you find a new café with vegan pancakes, when you see a car with an anti-fur bumper sticker, when you find stylish, leather-free shoes and they're not too expensive, either.

S is for Strident, at which your natural resting pulse is set and it is also for Skimming menus, which you could win an Olympic medal at, you are so nimble.

T is for Tofu, because it is common knowledge that you have it delivered by the semi-truckload weekly.

U is for Unfortunate example, which you probably were that first year or two, let's be honest. We all were.

V is for Vegan, what more can we say?

W is for Wanker, the British version of a Jackass.

X is for Xerox, which you blinded your corneas with when creating your first 'zine.

Y is for Yelp, the disgruntled vegan's playground.

Z is for ZZZZ, the sound you make while you are off dreaming of the ultimate snappy comeback to that kid or co-worker or cousin who makes stupid little comments about what you eat every damn time you see him like it's original or something.

Anyone have more words to add?

The Pleaser's Guide to Pissing People Off
Originally posted on Wednesday, May 26, 2010

It happened. You went and pissed someone off.

He may or may not think that you're a selfish, egotistical jerk. She may or may not think that you're a rude, thoughtless dolt. Oh, this person may or may not be thinking it, all right.

Despite this, I am reasonably certain that I can assure you all or most of the following: you will not be stabbed in the shower; squirrels and children alike will not heckle you as soon as you step outdoors; your heart will not rot from within because of your irredeemable vileness; the sun will not shrivel and dissolve into a sticky, boiling sludge because of all the international venom directed at you; there is no life-sized voodoo doll of your person with giant pins stuck all over it; your entire town will probably not turn their backs upon you in one collective, community-wide snub. If you are someone who likes to please, and those of us homo sapiens who are not sociopathic narcissists have this survival instinct to a greater or lesser extent, it can feel pretty cataclysmic sometimes when you know you've pissed someone off. Depending on the sort of home you grew up in, you might think that you can control the outcome of situations if only you avoid stepping on any toes. Don't talk to Mom before she's has her first cup of coffee; don't mumble around Dad. The problem is that you can't control most outcomes and in life, toes will be trod upon, intentionally and inadvertently. Sometimes the right thing to do is apologize. Sometimes, though, you will be expected to even if you didn't do anything wrong. Or you did do something "wrong" but it wasn't really wrong because it was well-intentioned, honest or unavoidable. This guide is for those times.

I'm going to go out on a limb here and assert that it's kind of good that you want to please. Kindness and sensitivity are good qualities. At the very least, society would be pretty unpleasant to live in if we all just lived by our own whims. You may have noticed something about those who don't care about pleasing others: they can be very unlikable. This is the sort of person who lacks empathy and compassion, who, if you were to say, "Hmm, you know, it rather hurts me when you try to run me over with your car," would say, "Really? Too bad because I enjoyed that and so I'm going to continue," as he gleefully puts the car in reverse to plow you over from a different direction. Not literally but figuratively. You are not this kind of person, despite the fact that someone might currently be pissed at you. The person who is pissed at you might make you feel like you tried to run him over with your car because, frankly, it might feel that way to him. You didn't. (Right? If you did, go loiter somewhere else.) What's an emotionally thin-skinned person to do when your natural instinct is to throw yourself on the ground and beg for forgiveness?

Give yourself a time-out

Take a moment. Let the feeling wash over you. The fear in the pit of your stomach, the jitteriness. You're scared of it? I understand. Still, sit with it without judgment. Give it a name: scared, nervous, rejected. The feeling gets worse if you try to ignore it or push it away. Feel it and release it. The reality of the situation is that it's not so awful, right? No rhinoceros is chasing you with steam coming out of his flared nostrils. You're likely feeling fear; the problem pleasers have is that of proportion. We take pissing people off to be much more monumental than it probably needs to be. So take a time-out before you respond.

Keep things in perspective

Was what you did really that bad? Was it intentionally hurtful? If it was, did it need to be said or done? Is it the end of the world? Remember that rhinoceros from above? I read something from a Buddhist monk once where he said that the height of suffering and pain is self-absorption. This is to say that when you lack perspective and connection, everything is life or death. We're uncentered. The fact of the matter is that the world keeps spinning. The sun rises and sets every day, even if your friend Nancy has been distant and the librarian gave you a dirty look for some inexplicable reason. Life goes on. Your monkey mind will chatter all kinds of nonsense into your ears if you let it. Instead, breathe in, breathe out...

Act as-if

Think of the most carefree person you know, the one who seems to skip everywhere she goes, is quick to laugh, lives with an infectious joie de vivre. Let's call her Didi. Imitate her. When you have pissed someone off and it's not really your fault but your stomach still hurts and your throat is all dry, imitate Didi. What does it feel like inside to be Didi? Kind of awesome, right? Even if it is all an illusion, even if Didi is hopped up on happy pills and punches her pillows at night, imitate the illusion.

Talk it out

Call a neutral friend, one who is supportive of you but also honest. Ask if you could have a little bit of her time while you talk through an issue with her. If she's a real friend, she'll be honored that you care about her opinion. Try to present the situation with fairness and as much honesty as you can muster. Chances are, you'll feel at least 63 times better after talking to a friend. You'll have perspective; your burden will be lighter.

Be gentle with yourself

The pleaser's natural impulse often is to add to the pile-on. "He's right! I am a no good, self-centered loudmouth. He forgot to add that I am also impatient and worthless. Let me add that to the list." Somehow we have the notion that beating ourselves up is necessary, even purifying. It's not. It's just adding an extra coat of pain that you don't need. Why not turn that desire to please inward a little? Be gentle and kind to yourself. Don't accept meanness, least of all from yourself. Give yourself an extra iced tea, take a walk after dinner, go to the beach. A little gentleness goes a long way.

Write it out

Writing out your feelings can be very cathartic. Allow yourself to write without editing, without your inner-critic. Just write it out, warts and all, and tear it up or burn it. Imagine your worries dissolving as the paper disappears.

Do not apologize!

If you have clarity that you did nothing wrong, please don't apologize. Even if you're just apologizing to get someone off your back, it causes harm to your self-esteem (and gives a bully a sense of victory) if you apologize for something you didn't do wrong. It sucks to say, "I'm sorry you feel that way," but sometimes that's the best you can do. Apologizing when you didn't do anything wrong is like apologizing for existing. Be kind, be compassionate, but don't do it!

Ask questions and learn

Is there something to take away from the experience? Are you gravitating toward people who demand apologies a lot? Are you someone who miscommunicates a lot and creates misunderstandings? What could you have done different? What could you do different in the future? Calm your mind and see what emerges.

To sum up: if you did something wrong, apologize, If you didn't, don't. In any case, the world will keep spinning, gravity will still be in effect, and no angry mob is likely going to chase you out of town with flaming sticks.

It's time to move on.

WHEN VEGANS (ALMOST) RULE THE WORLD

This Artisan Life
Originally posted on Monday, May 16, 2011

The other day, I saw a sign on North Avenue promoting the "hand-pattied" hamburgers a restaurant offered and something clicked in the back of my mind. Later that day, it really sunk in when I saw an ad referring to an ice cream shop with hand-scooped cones. As it could be both tricky and unhygienic to scoop ice cream with one's feet or elbows, this is an important detail to bring to a potential customer's attention. I also realized that restaurants and artisan food merchants alike are quick to point out all the handmade, personal touches they bring to their work. Why don't I? I don't give myself nearly enough credit for all the things I do in this life of mine. I create countless artisan, handcrafted moments every single day.

The above paragraph, for example, was self-punctuated as are all the sentences that follow. Every word I select will always be crafted with my own synapses and typed by my own hands in-house: they have not turned over to an impersonal third party in any part of their journey to the screen. As I write, I am also sipping hand-poured local water prepared with house-made ice cubes that were produced in small batches in a glass that I choose myself among many others for how its form fits my unique hand. On that topic, machine generated, commercial ice cubes lack that certain flair, don't you think, one looking exactly like the next? I would just as soon put toxic sludge in my glass than I would outsource my ice cubes. My ice cubes are as individualized as snowflakes. I honor them and I grieve when they are selected to chill my beverages. I do not take these things lightly. As a side note, if you are to drink chilled beverages, I suggest that you have the courage to hand-prepare and select your own ice cubes. If you cannot do this, I suggest that you please ask your ice merchants the process that went

70

into making the cubed frozen water they sell. It could be an eye-opening experience.

Making my own ice cubes is one small commitment I make in order to create a detail-driven, handmade life. Let's look at a typical but utterly organic day in my life…

After arising, I make my own bed, and, as I do every day, I hand-smooth the sheets and I self-fold the top of the comforter back just so. When I get dressed, my clothes - previously folded and sorted by hand - are chosen based on the temperature and my activities of the day and only then are they placed on my body. By hand, of course. When I exercise, I self-lift all my own weights and am responsible for generating my own motion. The sweat, of course, issues from my own pores that have been exfoliated by hand. My dental care, face cleaning, shower and house-prepared blended drink, of course, are done with myself and replete with this same spirit of autonomy and exquisitely rigorous attention to detail.

It is exhausting to think about, I know, and I haven't even tied my own shoelaces with my singular bow (secured in the middle with two loops and the ends hanging loose) and walked my naturally conceived, self-gestated, and then umbilically-, mammory-, hand- and then finally self-nourished son to school. While my partially-free-range son is at school - in the district of the house that we selected after personally touring many others by foot, of course – more thoughtfully handcrafted work needs to be undertaken.

My day continues with more self-constructed sentences and the occasional personally guided Internet expedition for research and entertainment purposes. Micro- and house-brewed homemade iced tea produced with local water is also replenished throughout the day and lunch is foraged from my own kitchen and self-tended garden, comprised usually of personally selected, hand-washed, -peeled and –prepared local organic produce. Then it is back to writing again, except when I need to personally compose messages to send to my correspondences. It is not easy but I wouldn't have it any other way.

WHEN VEGANS (ALMOST) RULE THE WORLD

When my son returns from school, I continue his education by reviewing his homework and home-schooling him until it is complete. Snacks are prepared and plated by hand, of course, and based on whatever items are available that day. Juice is locally purchased, home-and hand-poured.

Dinner. So much handcraftedness, all prepared in small batches, too exhausting to detail…

After dinner, the table is cleared off by hand and the dishes are hand-rinsed and-loaded into the dishwasher. The floor is then swept by hand and items that have been carried elsewhere are placed back into their designated areas. The cat's litter box is hand-scooped. As we are a family that prioritizes the DIY philosophy, we do our own dental care, maintain our own skin and so forth in house. At bedtime, we turn back our own sheets, read to ourselves and/or to each other, and then cease sensory activity for the day and pursue a state of reduced consciousness. We do this all on our own. Although it is not easy, we wouldn't have it any other way. It is the way of the artisan, after all.

How have you handcrafted your life today, friends?

The Sand Dollar
Originally posted on Friday, January 28, 2011

Last March, my mother moved in with us. It was a long, circuitous path from her living independently to moving into our brick bungalow but the trajectory to our home has also been obvious for years. My mother giving up her place was not something any of us wanted but, given the circumstances, it was working with the cards we were dealt in the best way that we could.

My mother was losing her wallet, her keys, forgetting to pick up her mail. This is a woman who had always prided herself on being so reliable and well organized (it skips a generation, apparently) that she has never paid a late fee in her life. Not for a late payment of a bill, not for an overdue library book because even if it was a ten-cent fine, that fine would be a black mark of judgment against her, a poor reflection upon her as a member of society.

When she started to decline more sharply, what was most telling to me was that she became blasé about the things most characteristic of her – orderliness, organization, being dependable – to the point where I was the one darting around her place, looking through drawers filled with dozens of unused spiral notebooks and under the bed for library books that were due. Also, as the easiest of easy targets, I had feverish visions of someone horrible following her home from her daily walk to her usual haunts – the pharmacy, the sandwich shop - and slipping into the building behind her. There were so many other concerns, too: She couldn't be trusted to take her medication right, she couldn't figure out how to use the phone, I was worried about her remembering to turn off her stove. When it came time to make the decision to move her in with us, it was an easy one. The decision was easy: the living together, that is the hard part.

People inevitably ask me why we didn't try assisted-living.

WHEN VEGANS (ALMOST) RULE THE WORLD

Simple: she is not able to care for herself enough to be accepted into one. Why not a nursing home, then? They have activities for residents, she would at least be around people closer to her age. My mother is fuzzy about a lot of things these days, but one thing she is very clear on is that she desperately does not want to go into a nursing home and I think her instincts are right on this one. I have seen her in those environments and she becomes very anxious, scared and uncomfortable. She is still lucid enough to know what a nursing home would mean for her. Although that is likely on the future horizon, we'd like to delay that as long as possible as it will be the end for her.

We've had to learn all about medications this year and how they interact, that all chairs need to be pulled out and pushed in, that when my mother gets even a simple cold everything falls apart, that becoming distracted in the grocery store could result in her filling her cart with bags of frozen shrimp that I will never cook in a million years, that "the red thing" means her purse and "the white paper" is usually a piece of mail (we still don't know what "the yellow thing" is), that if we don't take out her hearing aids for her, she will put them wherever (check the mantel first), that she cannot simply go to bed without a whole, elaborate ritual.

My husband is a thick-skinned, patient type of person, a typically stoic Minnesotan who manages to also be kind and nurturing. In other words, he's a much better person than I. When it's one's own parent, though, our buttons are much more easily pushed. One effect of my mother's condition means that even though I work very hard to care for her, I still get treated like a shady sixteen-year-old who is asking for the car keys again whenever I try to carve out time for myself. It's like the old dynamic between us remains intact, frozen in time. Even when my husband is home with my mother, she expects me to keep to a curfew and despite how this activates every last rebellious synapse I have, I've learned to roll my eyes and abide by it or I will be pestered to the breaking point.

This year, I have learned all about pyrrhic victories, how to identify them and, when I have the self-discipline, how to walk away from them. Sometimes, though, it takes every last bit of resolve. In those moments, when my own nerves seem to have been lit on fire like the wick on dynamite, I try to imagine myself as Wonder Woman or Supergirl in a bright red cape and leotard, able to deflect anything life tosses my way with my handy wristlets. This helps somehow, even while I know that I'm still the one standing there, wristlet-free, squeezing my hands into tight, clenched balls.

It is not always bad. Most weekdays consist of her napping and watching games shows or judges squinting at defendants in TV courtrooms. I sit in the sunroom and I write, edit, read, research and generally try to lose myself in words. Mornings and evenings are our rough times, trying to get my son ready for school when my mother wants her medication, trying to get him calmed down for bed when my mother's television blares in the other room. Our clash of lifestyles and the very different temperaments we were born with has not brought out the best in me in such close quarters. All it takes is for one seemingly minor, mundane irritant (my mother eating potato chips – gah! Another irritation! - out of the bag instead of a bowl, for example, leaving crumbs everywhere and why-oh-why of all those lifelong traits she abandoned did neatness have to among them?) to send me spiraling. It's not the crumbs, of course, or the potato chips: it's everything. It's never having taken care of herself so she'd have a stronger foundation, it's losing my personal space, it's rearranging everything in our lives, it's the lack of privacy, it's the helplessness, it's still being treated like a juvenile delinquent in my forties even when I was never one to begin with, which brings me back to all the old baggage. It's funny how potato chips can do that to a person.

Caring for a chronically unwell parent whose best hope is to not get worse can bring out parts of yourself that you'd rather prefer remain dormant or at least hidden.

75

WHEN VEGANS (ALMOST) RULE THE WORLD

Over holiday break, when my mother was in Texas visiting my aunt for three weeks, we had the a chance to go away, to run for the hills or the valley or wherever the hell we could go that was far away from here, and we sprinted toward it with the panting enthusiasm of a pack of golden retrievers chasing after a ball at the beach. And to the beach we headed: Florida, land of orange groves and amusement parks and palm trees and miniature golf and fundamentalists and Jews and pelicans and the Atlantic Ocean. No medication that needed to be dispensed, at least not by our hands. No litter box that needed to be scooped and no sidewalks that needed to be shoveled by us either. The only chairs we needed to push out or in would be our own. We were going to Florida. Three trilling syllables rolling off the tongue, a happy song, a stone skipping on the water before it sinks to the ocean floor to hang out with the starfish: Flor-i-da.

The snow on the ground in southern Georgia was the first sign that it wasn't exactly blisteringly hot in the Sunshine State but it was a lot warmer than Chicago. It did not matter. We were away. My husband and I immediately fell into our natural rhythm of traveling together – basically, research where the vegetarian restaurants are and then let the interesting points in between them become the little dash marks – and our son was more than amendable to it. We became that unit of three again that functions so well together.

On our second day in Florida, we were on the beach in St. Augustine, a place with a name that sounds as far away from Chicago as possible, the first time my son had seen the ocean since he was four. There were shells everywhere we looked and it was finally warm enough to cuff our parts and walk into where the tide had just pulled away. We started instinctively putting shells in our pockets for my son's classmates, squatting down to examine the radius around us, the foamy water fizzing over rocks. Strange brown birds unknown to me ran on skinny legs along the tide, a kite bobbed nearby, children climbed on the rocks like billy goats. It was during one of those moments when

I was crouching in the sand on the balls of my feet, reaching for shells with my son and husband in the near distance when I thought, This is peace. I hadn't felt that way in years, the feeling of not having any responsibilities or expectations, just of pure enjoyment and being. It was amazing to me with what ease I could transition into beachcomber mode, to being someone who only cared about where the next interesting shell might be found. The only thing that occupied me was plucking my fingers through the sand like nimble tentacles.

After an hour or two, we needed to leave to find a hotel. Walking back, something brought me farther out to where the tide had just rolled out and I crouched again over the popping foam, unable to resist the lure of more discoveries. As I was about to take a step, I crouched again, noticing a small off-white circle in the sand that looked like a drawing of a flower with a stick. Pushing the sand away, I kept digging until my fingers were around a big, perfect sand dollar. Five notches exactly under the flower's petals, a small star in the middle, a loopy etching of a flower shape on the back, elegant symmetry. Even when I was holding it, turning it around in my hands, I was in disbelief, my jaw open as if I'd just seen a mermaid splashing in the waves.

I am a city girl by choice and temperament. I marvel at architecture daily, at the diversity of accents and faces around me when I'm on the train, at the crackling, robust energy all around me. It's not so often that I'm given the opportunity to be blown away by the simple, magnificent design of a sand dollar discovered by my own eyes. I'm the sort of person who always looks up a second too late to see a falling star, who catches the merest glimpse of yellow feathers before a gold finch darts away. Nature's magic show is going on out there, I know it, but it's always been elusive to my own eyes. Here was something perfect in my hand, something labored over, a home designed out of necessity but artfully crafted without any shortcuts.

What I held in my hand was the sun-bleached skeleton of a sea urchin, the protective bone a spiny animal once covered before the evolutionary drive compelled him to become burrowing creature. The scratchy flower shape is created by the sand dollar's tube-shaped feet, which are used for breathing. There are scientific explanations for the design and symmetry of a sand dollar, having to do with respiration, gas exchange and evolution. The thought that a spiny sea urchin would work so hard to find food, survive and fight the current - young ones are even thought to ingest sand to better plant themselves to the ocean floor – and still leave behind a work of beauty without expecting a word of praise from its aquatic community kind of impresses me. Just by living, they create a beautiful home in the process, a natural by-product of life itself.

I finally held up the sand dollar, unable to stop grinning, and my son and husband came running toward me, whooping. I could barely speak. Whenever I looked at my son sitting in the back seat of the car for the rest of our vacation, most likely he was turning that perfect disk around in his hands, staring at it in that wide-eyed way he has about him.

Sometimes life can be really, really challenging. We're just trying to get through our day, get from Point A to Point B, and we're sent spinning. We're without an anchor, we can't see where we're going, we're drowning in it all. Burrowing in, though, we can create a beautiful life as something to leave behind. Maybe no one else will ever notice or appreciate it. Maybe our lives will just look messy and confusing and unnecessarily challenging to other people. Maybe it'll look that way to us, too. At our best, though, we know what we're doing. We're digging in and building beautiful lives as if there were an evolutionary drive toward it. A beautiful life is not one without dark, petty, horrible moments and breakdowns. It is seeing our shortcomings, looking at them without fear, and trying to do better, trying to etch pretty little flowers on ourselves just because.

I'm working at it. Sand dollars don't happen overnight, either.

The Zombievore's Dilemma

Wednesday, February 9, 2011

Zombievore: *An omnivore as the walking dead; an automaton.*

From the outset, let me just say that I don't think that all omnivores are pernicious zombies without measurable brain waves. Clearly, that would be unfair, the sort of absurd overstatement people love to point to as further evidence of mean-spirited, wrong-headed vegan, feminist sedition. Of course I am not claiming that all omnivores are zombies, just a sizable percentage that has not been calculated yet. By Zombievores, I am referring to individuals who are not using the complex reasoning skills they were presumably born with and are instead idling, aided by their built-in societal privileges and tendency to allow others to do their thinking for them. An omnivore who has abandoned his or her critical thinking faculties in favor of meaningless word repetition and habituated practices, who lurches through life without regard for those who do not share the same privileges, is maintaining a Zombievorous lifestyle. If this description doesn't fit you, then please, no need to be offended.

There are various categories of Zombievores. There are the **Fast Food Zombievores**, of course. There are the **Custom-Fixated Zombievores**, too. These first two types are easy to identify and avoid, unless one should happen to live within your own home. There is a classification of Zombievore that is usually more subtle and cunning than the others, though. They are best known for their ability to penetrate and assimilate into otherwise progressive spheres of society with a message that captivates and seems to be imbued with the spirit of positive change but, upon closer inspection, simply reinforces the established order. These Zombievores are generally affluent, urban, well educated and Caucasian though there are certainly exceptions, and their undisputed leader is Michael Pollan. To understand him and

79

the particular sway he has over his order of Zombievores, one must first get a recap of his recent visit to one of Oprah Winfrey's famous chairs.

Have you ever gone to a party that you're a little apprehensive about but your friends have been building it up in your head all week so you think that you should stop being such a sour crab apple all the time and just go with the flow? It might be decent, it might even be worthwhile, you think to yourself, psyching yourself up like the pompom girl you never were. You arrive at the party, though, and you can see from the start that it's pretty much what you already expected and feared: vacuous chitchat that you fail at both initiating and maintaining. Joyless tittering back and forth.

"It will be okay," you tell yourself. You remind yourself to smile, to unclench your shoulders, to get a drink. It's still early. The party hasn't hit its stride yet. Then you notice an energy shift in the room and you see him.

He's surrounded by disciples who chuckle as if on cue at his bon mots. When he is speaking of something poignant, the devotees mirror his sincerity, leaning in, nodding, creasing their foreheads with concern. When he is articulating his opinion, it is with the mien of an authority, and if the others surrounding him could, they would start taking notes. Despite the adoration, he considers himself to be humble, earthy even, and despite the salary he draws and his impressive résumé, he is one of the little people, at least in his own mind.

At this point, any shadow of the doubt is instantly erased. You're almost relieved because you now have proof positive that, indeed, nothing good can come of this assembly. This is because Michael Pollan is in the room and he is a Very Special Guest. This was the experience of watching Oprah's "Let's try on a new lifestyle this week like a new pair of awesome, pretty shoes!" – I mean - her thoughtful exploration of the vegan lifestyle with that avowed consumer of serenely, lovingly butchered animals,

Michael Pollan, curiously stuck to her side for the entire hour like a human barnacle in an expensive suit.

He is the Golden Prince of his particular classification of Zombievores, giving them sustenance and the drive to continue with his patently void nuggets of personal validation. Somehow his followers are able to extract enough from these little nuggets to sustain themselves but it is clear that they are not running on quality fuel. Too smart and ambitious to be a zombie himself, Michael Pollan has become wealthy writing books and telling affluent, greenish omnivores to keep doing what they're doing and telling aspiring affluent, greenish omnivores to do a better job (in other words, spend more money for ever-more exclusive animal products) at what they are doing. The stricken become . They repeat the catchphrases of their guru, dull-eyed and flat in tone, not an original thought firing their synapses: freeeee-raaaaaange, they lurch. Sus-taaaaaain-able, they growl. Graaaaaass-fed, they drone. Hu-maaaaaane, they bellow as they corner you in the room, humid, meaty breath in your face.

The Golden Prince of the Zombievores was planted by Oprah's side the entire episode, her wingman, a designer security blanket, the yuppie habit apologist anointed to sanction meat-eating by waving his glittery green magic wand and making everyone feel better, even righteous, with his platitudes that do not stand up to reason.

Zombievores have been rendered insensible by the willful suspension of disbelief that the Pollanization process requires. The Pollanated have decided to stop thinking because it protects their privileges and they have elected to spout empty banalities instead that defy common sense.

"I want to help the small farmers," they will assert. As though one can't help small farmers who don't kill or exploit animals.

"It's my personal choice," the Zombievores will rail. Their supposed right to take another's life simply because they have the means and the privileges is the antithesis of a sound ethical argument. Next.

"It's sustainable," they will allege. For real? Given the amount of space these animals would naturally, normally claim in nature, it is a mathematical impossibility to provide the landmass these billions of beings would need thus we have concentrated feeding operations. Given human consumption habits and the lack of adequate landmass to support that, any allegedly sustainable animal product is a luxury item produced for a relatively elite, affluent few. The Pollanated plan is clearly an untenable model for meeting demand, thus it is willful ignorance. Given the sheer amount of animal products people consume, the only model for meeting demand is an industrial one, and that doesn't sit right with Mr. Pollan and his adherents who vastly prefer an aesthetic of exclusivity. It doesn't matter if his model is steeped in an illogical, idealized reality: the fairy tale is all that matters here. A drastic reduction in consumption is the only way that this model could realistically function.

"The animals do not suffer," they will claim. Because getting a bolt in the skull, a knife slashed across the throat or a bullet in the brain always feels fabulous, especially when it is unnecessary. Being forcibly impregnated, getting their milk stolen from them, their babies taken from them and often killed, having their ears notched for identification purposes because we enjoy exercising our personal choice to enjoy their "product" is unkind. *Pollanated Zombievores* are loath to admit this and even more loath to admit that these are standard practices on many of the beloved, pastoral small farms they believe in with the blind trust of a child putting a tooth under her pillow in anticipation of a winged Tooth Fairy.

So Zombievores. They walk among us. You will find them at the farmers market, at the bookstore, at fundraisers and at the beach. They are everywhere.

To put it plainly, if you value your time, your best defense is to simply walk away. Engaging the afflicted tends to yield scant rewards though even the most seasoned of us occasionally will forget this cardinal rule and attempt to break through. Pollanated Zombievores have everything to lose with honestly evaluating their deliberately cultivated naïveté – their ethics, their creature comforts, their privileges, their integrity and character – and so they must maintain their position at all costs, even if it makes no sense.

If you feel that you have the time to spare, by all means, it is your prerogative to engage such a Zombievore. Remember that they are thwarted by logic and reason. Don't be scared. The thing about the Pollanated variety of zombie is that they don't want to eat your brains: they only want to eat heirloom quality, rare, specialty, sloooooow-foooooood-approved brains. You should be fine.

Concerned that you might actually be among the stricken? Ask yourself some questions: Have you referenced the "snout-to-tail" movement without irony or wanting to vomit? Do you fetishize the ovum of your backyard hens? Is your quest for obscure, artisan quality paté leaving you exhausted, stressed out and broke? Do you become anxious when you are fresh out of bone marrow for spreading on your morning baguette? Do you feel an ever-escalating pressure within the ranks of your friends to consume possibly life-threatening viscera in order to fit in? If so, you may very well be a Pollanated Zombievore.

I don't claim to be an expert in the field of Pollanated Zombievore recovery, but my recommendation is to stop immediately because, seriously, you are tedious. You must simply put yourself on a strict diet of avoiding the works and wisdom of Michael Pollan. Those first few weeks are the most critical and they will undoubtedly be the most rough. The old friends will try to lure you back with promises of nouveau butcher shops, charcuterie and out of the way barbecue joints. If you feel the old bloodlust rise up inside you again, grab a beet, drink some cranberry juice. Fill your home and body with fresh produce.

WHEN VEGANS (ALMOST) RULE THE WORLD

Spend some time outdoors, breathe in the fresh air. Take notice of the birds, the dogs, the squirrels, how they live simply for their own reasons, not for our purposes. Think of how much free time you have to actually bring good into the world now that your brain waves have started to fire up again and original thoughts have begun trickling in. Imagine how liberated you will feel when you're no longer lurching from meat counter to meat counter, shoveling internal organs into your mouth.

You know that you are free when believing self-serving fairy tales has lost its appeal, when empty platitudes ring hollow and critical thinking has been restored. You are free when you recognize that your fleeting desires and tastes do not have primacy over another being's right to live. At this time, the process of Pollanization will have been reversed.

You're welcome.

The Personal is Political: Veganism is a Feminist Act
Originally posted on Friday, November 2, 2012

"The moment we begin to fear the opinions of others and hesitate to tell the truth that is in us, and from the motives of policy are silent when we should speak, the divine floods of light and life no longer flow into our souls." Elizabeth Cady Stanton

I was born a feminist. I'm not sure where it came from – perhaps my dynamo of a grandmother, confident to the core – but growing up, I never thought that I was anything but a complete equal to everyone else. I was a natural feminist and when I learned that there were was a real need for it - that there were those who believed in arbitrary, illogical and repressive hierarchies - the fire within me to correct injustices was found its fuel source. When I saw kids throw rocks at squirrels, heard people make bigoted remarks, witnessed others being treated unfairly, my hands would involuntarily ball up into tight little fists. Even if I wanted to keep quiet, to not attract the ire of that bully down the block who threw rocks at the squirrels or the loudmouth at the bar years later, I physically couldn't do it. It'd be like asking a volcano to please not explode. My feminism and my passion for equality and fairness were always fully interwoven and integrated.

Now here is the sad part, the whole falling out between me and mainstream feminism that left me so disappointed. I will concede that maybe I'm naïve. It's quite possible that I'm just out-of-synch with the world around me. I have come to accept that I am stubbornly idealistic sometimes. This is all possible.

But…

When I came of age as a feminist in college the idea of intentionally adopting a patriarchal system of oppression was unthinkable. This is not to say that I was perfect by a long

85

shot: I have a virtual walk-in closet chock full of skeletons just accumulated from the Booze Era of my life that lasted from ages 19 to 26. Even with a mean hangover, though, the idea was that I was trying to dismantle vicious systems of tyranny, not benefit from them. The thought of consciously participating in a fundamentally unjust and violent power structure once I knew about it would have been akin to keeping slaves simply because I could.

Animal agriculture is a historically and essentially oppressive one, one that asserts at its very root that "what's yours is mine" if you don't happen to be a human. Your milk, your eggs, your life. This is an entrenched patriarchal conceit, born of domination, and the idea that women, feminists at that, would accept this particular status quo is strange and troubling to me. That they would adopt it and wrap it in the parlance of quasi-feminist empowerment is especially unsettling. Yet I see photos of women with weapons standing over dead animals, grinning victoriously. I read grandiloquent accounts of slaughter, including one in which a woman was quoted as saying that she felt like "a goddess, an Amazon" after killing a chicken with her own hands. (Oh, and a knife.) I hear women speaking with obvious pride about shooting deer, killing the animals they have raised, taking them apart from limb to limb. Less overtly inspired by bloodlust, I know of avowed feminists who could "never" give up "their" cheese, who don't pause to reflect on the lives of the chickens on the plate in front of them at their favorite Thai restaurant, who say that they consider their preferences first as a matter of self-empowerment.

Here is the thing: when feminists are accepting and embracing the tools of oppression, it's time to reevaluate things. Ladies, you have co-opted your own feminist principles and replaced them with maintaining your comforts instead.

Feminism is a social justice movement, one that asserts at its core that females are equal to males. No one deserves violence, injustice, suppression, and inequality simply because she was born with X and Y chromosomes, just as no Jews deserve persecution just because of the lineage they were born into or people of color deserve it because they are not Caucasian. We know this. Why are the animals people exploit and kill – those who were born to circumstances outside of their own control, just like all others – excluded from the sphere of consideration by otherwise thoughtful, kind, and progressive people? Because unrestricted access to animals is their right, damn it, and they will guard this privilege to the finish.

Feminism is about many things and it differs from interpreter to interpreter. I get that. If feminism implies through word and deed (or is also complicit by the lack thereof) that some females are more equal than others, though, this crosses into the troubling mentality that supports slavery and selective, self-serving habits over moral consistency. When females of different species are forcibly impregnated and have their babies and milk taken from them in an enforced cycle of pregnancy and birth until they are considered worthless, that is a crime against them and it is gendered. This is institutionalized, state-sanctioned violence and exploitation. Wouldn't a feminist naturally take a stand against such abuse? Wouldn't a feminist naturally not aid and abet such heinous cruelty? Wouldn't a feminist naturally disavow such distinctly unenlightened and unnecessary violence?

I am a feminist because I believe that all beings were created equal. I am a feminist because I reject the common practices of patriarchal violence, no matter how culturally ingrained they are and beneficial they might be to me. I am a vegan because I am a true blue, proud feminist. We have to be honest to ourselves and honest to each other: are those of us who believe in social justice going to go the distance for others or are we just going to remain in our own comfort zone? Are we going to be fearless as we create this new world order or are we going to accept business as usual, choosing comfort over challenging ourselves to be true champions for sovereignty of the body and spirit?

WHEN VEGANS (ALMOST) RULE THE WORLD

Despite how disappointed I have felt by other feminists over the years, I am still one in my heart and soul. This won't ever change. I am just ready for other feminists to step up to the plate and take the animals off of it. We have to never let go of a commitment to tenacious compassion.

We are the ones. The future of the world rests in the hands of the powerful and fearless vegan feminists.

The Persistence of Fairy Tales

Originally posted on Friday, August 31, 2012

"Peace is a process of retraining the mind to process life as it is, rather than as you think it should be." Dr. Wayne Dyer

When I was a child, one of my favorite books was a lavishly illustrated collection of Hans Christian Anderson's fairy tales; the story I liked most of all was The Emperor's New Clothes and not just because of the image of the pompous central character strutting around in his underwear. The story is about a narcissistic emperor duped by two swindlers posing as weavers who decide to capitalize on his vanity and convince him that they could make him a suit of such exquisite materials that it actually has magical properties: it is such finery that it will be only be visible to those who are worthy of its fine quality. The weavers actually have no cloth but they make a great show for days out of the measuring, cutting, and weaving of this supposedly magnificent material and the emperor sends his officers to check on the progress of the suit they are making. The statesmen, afraid of seeming inferior by admitting that they don't see anything, each report back to the emperor, gushing about the surpassing grandeur of the suit he has commissioned. Privately, though, they are each deeply troubled, believing that they are the only ones who can't see or feel a thing as the weavers work on their invisible garment.

When it is time for the emperor to display his magical suit in a procession for the townspeople, the weavers again make a great show of putting the invisible-to-all suit on him, pulling it up his arms and legs, standing back to admire it, while everyone, including the emperor, praises its unparalleled quality, each afraid to admit to themselves and each other that they do not see a thing. When the emperor finally does the procession, the townspeople, all informed of the supposed properties of the suit and afraid of looking stupid or beneath their neighbors, make a great public display of being astonished by its beauty. The charade continues until a child, unaware that everyone else was participating in this unspoken deception, impulsively shouts out the obvious, that the emperor isn't wearing any clothes. Soon, the townspeople abandon the ruse and the crowd yells that the emperor is wearing no clothes. Even as it dawns upon him that he had been deceived by the weavers, the vain emperor must continue, now humiliated and stripped of self-delusion, parading in front of the villagers in his undergarments while everyone knows that he has been made a fool.

This story appealed to me not only because of the moral about the silliness of vanity and ego but also the concept of clinging to a belief despite all the clear evidence that it is a false one. Like the emperor, when we want to believe a lie about ourselves, we cling to the self-deception even more resolutely, sometimes as if our lives depended on it being true.

For the past 17 years, I have heard otherwise intelligent people tell me fantastical tales with a straight face as a means to justify their omnivorous habits. I have heard time after time that plants feel pain, despite having no central nervous system or this notion having no evolutionary logic. Just a few days ago, someone ventured that mowing a lawn was akin to trimming a dog's nails. I have heard people who in no other ways emulate indigenous people invoke their "respect for Native Americans" as a way to infuse their meat-eating with an air of quasi-spirituality. (Along those lines, I have heard enough people wax philosophic about the Circle of Life - and their role in the death part of it – to fill the liner notes of every Kansas and Moody Blues album ever pressed.) I've heard people claim that they "climbed to the top of the food chain" as if they have fur and blood under their own fingernails. I have heard people insinuate that caring for animals means that you do not care for humans, as if the two cancel each other out, as if we are only allotted a measurable, finite amount of compassion. I've had many people express concerns to me about "What would happen to all the animals?" if the world went vegan, as if the process would happen overnight. I have even had someone tell me once that her "totem animal is a tiger and her tiger needs meat." Yes, she said this with a straight face. Yes, I almost bit through my lower lip to not burst out laughing.

Despite the occasional person with a ravenous, bloodthirsty tiger lurking within, it's interesting to me how little the excuses have changed over the years. In other words, the same justifications people told me in 1995, they are still repeating. One thing has changed, though. One very damaging narrative has been adopted wholesale by society at large that wasn't there before. The new conceit is that the animals conscientious people eat are "humanely raised and slaughtered." [I will cease the quotation marks here and trust that the reader knows that every time I say humane that this is not my view.] The spin is that the images we see of beings suffering in confinement are not telling the whole story: this is just the worst of the worst. That's not all the animals. There is a verdant, wildflower-filled meadow somewhere out there where the animals gambol and the noble farmer dwells with his family in a farmhouse. This is what all those who are conscientious meat-eaters consume. All of them. It just so happens that despite smaller farms representing a very, very small percentage of the industry – the USDA's own census shows that more than 99% of animals come from industrial settings - somehow, as if wishful thinking made it true, humanely procured animal products is all that everyone eats. In the house and out of the house. For breakfast, lunch and dinner.

This essay is only tangentially about the great deception of humane animal products. Regardless of where the animals people eat were born, they all face a knife and/or bolt to the brain needlessly in the end and that is all I need to know. They are still exploited from birth to death as if they and their bodies were our birthright. Their babies are still stolen from them for our purposes. It is still enslavement. I don't want to write about that today, though.

WHEN VEGANS (ALMOST) RULE THE WORLD

I have written a lot about the exploitation of animals through the lens of compassion but right now the concept of critical thinking is driving me. How is it that we willfully suspend our disbelief when the facts do not line up with something that we want to face despite how glaringly obvious it is? And how did we get to the point where virtually all of society effectively co-signs on this self-deception, holding onto the fabrication more tightly than someone clinging to a log in the Colorado River?

When I ask how the mathematical impossibility of free-range could happen on our limited landmass given consumption habits, I am met with the equivalent of hands over the ears, "La-la-la, I can't hear you!" antics. When I say that this wouldn't occur without a drastic, and I mean drastic, reduction in consumption, I get blank stares. When I say that eating any animal products regardless of its label is enormously taxing to our planet and wasteful of resources, eyes glaze over. When I say that if everyone ate the way that the foodie elite does, it'd be disastrous, I get diversionary tactics. When I say that eating animals is unnecessary and it necessarily causes pain and death, far-fetched hypothetical scenarios are repeated to me as if they were accurate representations of reality.

Why have people bought into the lie of humane slaughter so fully that they are willing to sacrifice the integrity of their critical thinking? Because it benefits them to maintain their privileges and to not think that they are jerks in the process.

I don't think that omnivores are all jerks, I really don't. That's silliness. To me, the steadfast clinging to fairy tales tells me something refreshing about the core of humanity - that we want to believe that we are good people because we want to be good people - and it tells me something positive about what we think about eating animals as the status quo. It tells me that people are uncomfortable with the act of eating animals at its root and this kernel holds a lot of hope for me. It also tells me that when animal advocacy organizations spin a narrative of "You can be vegan, you can be an omnivore, or you can pick what's behind Door #3" and what's behind that door is the promise of a clear conscience without changing any beloved habits, we are getting into the shameful territory of marching animals to their deaths. The human urge to believe in false narratives when presented with an ugly truth is just too alluring for most to resist. When the rest of society is deeply invested in maintaining the fabrication, critical thinking short-circuits so quickly you can practically hear it happen.

I am a slow study, apparently: I was an omnivore for the first 15 years of my life, a vegetarian for 12 years after that, and, once I couldn't hide from it anymore, a vegan. Everyone has his or her own process and path and I respect that. Damn, though, I am glad that I didn't have anyone patting me on the back and spoon-feeding me reassuring stories that would prolong my self-deception when I was transitioning. Now this fairy tale has been inserted into the dialogue and the false notion of a victimless exploitation and killing has been woven over eyes everywhere. Don't get me wrong: I love fiction. I love it so much I wrote a whole book filled with it. I just don't like telling fiction that justifies killing others.

Despite being portrayed as society's dreamers and tree-huggers, pie-in-the-sky idealists and fantasists, those of us who unwaveringly refuse to pretend that using and eating animals is harmless are actually the ones who are facing reality. We are the ones pointing at the products of death and oppression and stating it for what it is. The people who are coming up with far-fetched and illogical excuses are the escapists, valuing their fantasyland more than living honestly. Like the child watching the emperor in the parade, we are pointing out the obvious because we are no longer part of the mass deception.

Just because we wish something were so does not make it so. Killing an innocent unnecessarily is always wrong. We shouldn't be weaving fairy tales about life-or-death matters and we most certainly shouldn't be believing them.

The Universal Mother

Originally posted on Wednesday, May 4, 2011

Some mothers I have known...

There was the young mother who ran into the dressing rooms screaming "Ada! Ada!" when her toddler was missing at the department store. Five frantic minutes later, she was found playing with a doll in the toy section and her mother was on her knees, holding her daughter in a desperately grateful embrace. They seemed to melt together, the little girl smoothing her mother's hair like she was the child as her mother sobbed against her.

Just as vividly, I remember the mother walking toward me on the sidewalk at a street festival with her little boy, revelers all around us. In one horrible and totally ordinary moment, the mother's sudden shriek cut through the air: the hard candy her son was sucking on became lodged in his throat and this completely lively boy was a minute or two from choking to death. The crowd froze around them – What's happening? What's the matter? - and the woman thumped her son's back. The candy ball shot out and the boy started wheezing. She picked him up and deeply exhaled, her eyes squeezed shut as she held her son to her, another desperately grateful mother.

Just last summer, I was talking to a friend at a pool when she abruptly flung her cell phone onto the tile and, with a huge splash, dove in, fully dressed. I didn't realize it at the time but she'd jumped in after her five-year-old, who had gone under water. He didn't know how to swim. My friend surfaced with him seconds later, both gasping for air, her glasses floating a few feet away. She told me that she didn't let go of him for the rest of the day.

For me, there was that gasping moment when my normally cautious son got caught up in trick-or-treating mayhem and suddenly darted into the street before I had a chance to stop him. Racing after him, I screamed as loud as I could with my arms up in the air as a driver slammed on her breaks within a foot of him. With the next breath I took, this one with my son in my arms, I felt like every emotion that motherhood activated inside me was ringing and pulsing: the deep relief, the naked gratitude, the profound vulnerability. Also, the understanding that I was moments away from the worst kind of horror imaginable to a mother.

From a child's perspective, I distinctly remember that fear-in-the-pit-of-my- stomach feeling when I was separated from my mother as a three-year-old at the Museum of Science and Industry. I remember the disorientation, being lost in a dangerous sea of unfamiliar, hurrying legs going every which way, and feeling such utter relief when my mother's calves and shoes appeared, I thought my heart would explode. Although there are always exceptions, mothers and their children reach for each other, seek comfort in one another, do not feel safe if one is unexpectedly missing. This is natural.

One does not need to be human to feel the deep-seated instinct to protect her babies, to seek the warmth of one's mother. When animal advocates point out the obvious – that mothers and their babies suffer profoundly when they are separated, that harming one's baby causes emotional trauma to the mother – we are accused of anthropomorphizing. We are portrayed as having centers as squishy as marshmallows, as having naive, sentimental, childish minds. In fact, it is a cold biological imperative, not just an emotional one, that drives a mother to want to nurture and protect her young: entire species would be wiped out if not for a mother's instinct to defend her babies. I think, though, that it's highly arrogant and self-serving to presume that humans alone have an emotional stake in their babies' livelihoods.

Dairy cows, with a gestation of around nine months, have their calves taken from them shortly after birth, destined to become forcibly impregnated milk producers and cheap meat like their mothers if they are female, veal flesh if they are male. The dairy cows bellow and moan, as any mother would, calling for their lost babies. The mother cheetah my son and I saw driving predators from her vulnerable cubs in the "African Cats" movie had the same fierce devotion to her babies that any other mother would, putting her own safety on the line to protect them. Hens show a physical response when they sense that their chicks are in distress: their heart rates elevate, they cry out to them. It is natural for the hens to do this. They are not machines. To claim that emotions are the sole province of the human species is committing the very crime that animal advocates are accused of time and time again: it is sentimentalizing.

One also doesn't need to be a mother to be deeply driven to protect another. Long before I ever had a baby, I felt the same kind of adrenaline surge when someone intentionally whipped a hard rubber ball at my dog as I would have if he had done that same thing years later to my son. I chased that guy down the beach, screaming at him, and he ran away as if his life depended on it. Maybe it did. I'm a non-violent person, but you don't mess with the ones I love.

For Mother's Day, I propose that we honor this natural drive within all of us to protect the ones we love, the ones who depend on our consideration, by not consuming the products of exploitation and cruelty. This common thread of wanting our babies to thrive is natural and noble, a key part of our essential being. Whether we are men or women, children or adults, human or hen, that universal mother is in all of us. Let's celebrate without exploiting another innocent mother who had not only the autonomy of her body but also her babies stolen from her for our appetites. Let's connect to that profound mothering spirit that links us together. She wants her babies to be well and protected from harm. I think we can understand.

Happy Mother's Day to everyone.

On Never Growing Up
Originally posted on Thursday, April 25, 2013

I've been told my whole life that I'd give up or grow out of my convictions. Certainly, there are a lot of things I've grown out of, for example:

- Ding-Dong-Ditch and prank phone calls

- The Electric Company and my membership in the Sonny and Cher Fan Club

- Grape Fanta and Bubble Yum

- Black fingernail polish and purple hair dye

- Bad-for-me boyfriends and waking up with hangovers

These things come and go, as they should. The idea of dropping my core values like they are last year's embarrassing fashion trend, though, is something entirely different. I have been assured by people most of my life that I would do just that, though. Quite simply, they were wrong.

When I was fifteen and a new vegetarian, I was told in no uncertain terms that I would go back to meat the first time I really craved a hamburger, and I was told as a young feminist activist that when I eventually understood "how the world works," I would just learn to accept it. Neither of these predictions repeated to me as fact by so many people came true. At all. As a new vegan, I was told by countless people that I would abandon my veganism once it stopped being convenient and as a new mother, I was told that I wouldn't be able to sustain my goals of breastfeeding and cloth-diapering.

These gloomy forecasts were repeated to me in a matter-of-fact, confident manner by those who, by their own accounts, had tried and failed to maintain those same aspirations. People who had once been "like me" took it upon themselves to debrief me on my inevitable future defeat, letting me know that eventually, I would settle into a comfortable place of acquiescence with the Real World, just as they had. I'd be humbled. I'd realize that these were just impulsive, ill-considered whims. In the mean time, my puerile zest was kind of sweet and adorable.

There are some key designations society tries to affix to those who reject the status quo. One is that it is arrogant to do so, and another is that it is naive. There are some even more cynical insinuations about those of us who are guided by our values, implying that it means we are self-absorbed, rude, immature, attention-seeking. The skeptics can pull the "I was once like you so I can speak of this with authority" card to try to legitimize their opinions and get the final word. "I know better than you because I once was you," as one former vegetarian told me.

Why are people often so resentful of values-driven action? Why is our society so dead-set on trampling down those who are being led by their passions and values? Why do those of us with deep convictions ignite a desire in so many others to keep us in our place even if we are just minding our own business? What is behind this pessimistic drive?

I've been lucky enough to be able to reconnect with old friends in recent years and it's so interesting to me how many tell me the same thing after we've caught up with each other: "You haven't changed." Not in a negative way but in an admiring way. Even after becoming a mother, even after a few grey hairs, even when it can no longer be attributable it to naiveté, I am still who I always was. I can only wonder, though, why I wouldn't still be passionate about the things I cared about when they first knew me. What does this say about us, and society's expectations of us, as we mature beyond that first blush of our enthusiasm?

Our society considers idealism and convictions to be endearing but childish qualities that we will eventually grow out of, once the we've been disappointed too many times or had enough of life's hard lessons knock them out of us. There are those of us, though, who have been disappointed plenty and who have had lots of life experiences and yet we still retain our core values. Why are we perceived as such rarities? I have to say, I've only felt my beliefs and determination flourish over the years, the fire burning brighter as I check days off the calendar. Yes, the rougher edges that come with youthful zeal have been softened some, and I can certainly accept the complex nuances of human behavior more now than I did as a neophyte. Instead of knocking me down, though, life's turbulence just serves to make me less easily distracted and more focused on the things that excite me and bring me joy, which, naturally, includes some things people think I would have grown out of long ago. Do I have a preternatural discipline? An iron will? I wish I could say so but, no, I don't. I am just living proof that there is no reason that our unique ethical drives, as personal to us as our own fingerprints, should be expected to wither away over time. We still retain our fingerprints as we grow older. Why shouldn't we still have our unique passions?

I think that one belief that might age us most is accepting the false dichotomy that tells us that we must give up the things we love and compromise our values for what we believe we should be doing with our lives. Giving them up because of this faulty idea makes us cynical, older than our years, resentful and even suspicious of those who haven't. When I think of people who really thrived in their elder years - Georgia O'Keefe, Howard Zinn, Gandhi, Martha Graham, Studs Terkel as well as every senior with enduring, quirky, consuming passions - all I can think is, "Thank goodness they didn't tamper down their enthusiasm and drive in exchange for some slippers and an easy chair." Thank goodness for that.

I have not given up my values and convictions but even as they have become more nuanced and complex over the years, they have also become more heartfelt and integrated to who I am. They have also become more personal. Giving them up would be giving up essential parts of myself and that's not going to happen. They are still unfolding and ripening, too. I know that I am not alone with this.

Let's hear it for never growing up. Never, ever do it. The best things in the world depend on this.

AND OTHER HOPEFUL PROJECTIONS
FROM THE VEGAN FEMINIST AGITATOR – MARLA ROSE

The Upside of Anger

Originally posted on Wednesday, March 13, 2013

"Just like our organs, our anger is part of us. When we are angry, we have to go back to ourselves and take good care of our anger. We cannot say, 'Go away, anger, I don't want you.' When you have a stomachache, you don't say, 'I don't want you stomach, go away.' No, you take care of it. In the same way, we have to embrace and take good care of our anger." Thich Nhat Hanh

Most of us have a problem with accepting anger. This is completely understandable: anger fuels hatred and war. It harms and destroys. Anger has brought a lot of fear to many lives, including my own. Anger kills.

We associate anger with violence, destruction and a whole host of frightening things and it's for good reason. I will come out and admit it, though: I am, at times, angry. Very, very much so. Living in a world where billions of sensitive beings are brutalized and slaughtered, where girls in India are sold by their parents as terrified young brides, where West African children are kept as slaves in order for corporations to sell cheap candy bars at convenience stores: why on earth wouldn't I be angry? The things that anger me are a truly renewable resource: dead zones in the oceans, demeaning billboards, the culture that drives so many teen girls to self-loathing and eating disorders. Every day, I add something new or sharply underline an item on the list that already loops around the moon and back. I'm not ashamed to admit this.

At my core, though, I am essentially a happy person. Years ago, I made promise to myself that I would be happy and I am fortunate enough to have a particular predisposition that allows me to make good on that promise. The people who know me in person know that I love to laugh and have fun. If I had a dollar, though, for each time someone who does not know me called me angry based on my responses to the things that chip away at my heart, I could buy an island off Tahiti and fill it with my own private army of people who wave their angry fists at the sky all day long. What fun would that be, though?

How do I explain this seeming incongruity between the very real anger and equally real joy that I feel? I think that it comes down to how the anger is worked through: is it allowed to fester and warp us, forcing us to bend to it, or can we consciously work it out of ourselves, and, in the process, create something that makes the world just a little bit, or even a lot, better? Channeling anger into something that is productive - in other words, something that I consider necessary, expansive, helpful and worthwhile - makes me very happy; it's almost a process of wizardry. I swear, I see sparks sometimes. At its best, anger gives those of us who possess it access to a potentially transformative experience.

Almost all of the projects I've worked on that I am most proud of have germinated from that seed of anger, no matter how positive they become in the nurturing process. That seed of anger is rooted in a deep desire for creating something different, and that is how it flowers. Without the seed of anger, though, I don't know that I would have that initial drive to create change. Anger provides the fuel that I first need to get out of the inertia that despondency and helplessness fosters. Here is an example of my process: after seeing the success of a "humane meat" festival, and seeing it become less and less friendly toward vegans, I thought, "Why on earth don't we have a vegan festival in Chicago? There are lots of us! It's ridiculous that we don't have our own festival. That really ticks me off. Stupid happy meat! What could I do? What could I do? Damn it, I could help to start a vegan festival." It was with this initial flash of discontent and anger that Chicago VeganMania, our region's largest free festival of its kind, was born almost five years ago.

The downside of anger, I think, comes from misdirection, stagnation, or turning anger into violence against another or oneself. Stewing in anger without transforming it into conscious and productive creative action is what is destructive and where we go backwards. The time we need to feel that anger and find our pathways to transformation is essential to the process, though, and I fear that with society's negative messaging about anger, many will deny themselves the profound metamorphosis it offers us. Sitting with and simply allowing our anger, accepting it, is how we begin to harness and transform it. Where would we be as a society without the fury of Stonewall, without the white-hot gall of the Suffragettes, without the moral outrage of the Abolitionists? They weren't just screaming in the streets: they created newspapers, art and music. They influenced culture and helped nudge society toward progress. Yes, peace and rainbows have their place but so does discontent and we need to honor that. Maybe we would be where we are now, maybe those in power would have willingly ceded their privileges if given enough time. Should those who are oppressed and killed, though, be asked to wait while polite requests are considered? Should the dysfunctional power dynamic inherent in making such requests be reinforced?

What really transforms the world? Love. But to get to love, we need to start somewhere, and sometimes, it is in the bright, hot embers of anger where we find the spark that we need to turn despair into positive action. Don't be afraid of it. Cultivating a joyful life is the biggest way that we can influence others but a little anger has its place in getting us there.

The Sanity of Compassion

Originally posted on Thursday, June 14, 2012

Back when my son was two, I was bored to tears with reading him Lyle Crocodile all the time. One evening, I grabbed The Lorax from the bookshelf on a whim for our night-time reading ritual; I didn't know how much he would be able to take away from it but I was determined to avoid reading about the house on East 88th Street for just one night. My son was speaking a little at this age, not a lot yet, so I didn't know how much he would understand from a more complex book like The Lorax, but I desperately needed a change in the rotation.

We snuggled together and I was happily reading along until I got to the end, when the last Truffula tree was struck down. I suddenly heard a gasp. It came from my son. I turned to look at him and tears were streaming down his cheeks: "No more tees!" he cried, pointed at the page, his eyes wide. "No more tees!" I was in disbelief: I was so lost in the story myself I had no idea that not only was he following along, he was deeply engrossed. My son screamed and wailed. I quickly skipped ahead in the book to the page where the little boy was given the last Truffula seed by the Once-ler.

"See? It's okay," I said, trying to soothe him, still taken aback myself. "The boy can plant the seed. He can save the trees. He'll plant more." My son wasn't having it. I explained that it was just a book, it wasn't real, but he still sobbed himself to sleep that night, sniffling and his breath catching until he finally drifted off. When my husband came home that night, I was still shaken. I told him what had happened. "Well," he said, "on the bright side, it is probably not going to be any trouble getting him to embrace being vegan."

In the moment of learning that the last beautiful Truffula tree had been chopped down, my two-year-old felt the injustice of that action so personally that he cried out in pain and anguish, as if he himself had been struck with an axe. There was no separation between my son and the trees; as children do, he loved trees – they are mysterious, majestic, providing sanctuary for many creatures – and his reaction made sense. We should cry out when we see such senseless acts of destruction. Eight years later, my son is still viscerally empathetic to others who are vulnerable. This response is natural, normal and sane. I was reminded of this last weekend.

We had gone away with our network of Chicago area vegan families for our annual weekend out of town together. This year, we went to the Mad City Vegan Festival in Wisconsin, about 2 ½ hours from Chicago, in lovely Madison. My son and his friend, also a vegan, had wandered into one of the rooms while they were screening *Vegucated*. I have not seen it yet but there were some graphic scenes of cruelty to animals. Apparently it is a small part of the film but it made a big impression on the kids. My son and his friend were so upset they left the room, not able to keep watching the movie.

Before they left, they saw animals shoved into cages without any consideration. They saw slaughterhouses and tortured cows, chickens and pigs. It made their eyes well up and, afterward, it made them angry.

Not knowing they had seen the movie, I noticed them sitting at a nearby table, looking uncharacteristically subdued and sad. I sat down next to them and they told me about what they had seen, how upsetting it was to them.

"The animals are killed just for sandwiches and chicken nuggets," my son said. He has these soulful, dewy eyes that can rip my heart out, especially at moments like this.

WHEN VEGANS (ALMOST) RULE THE WORLD

"They just cram them into cages. They kill the pigs and then they shred them into bacon," said my son's friend, shaking his head. "Baconism has to end!"

"It's not worth it, is it?" I said.

"No!"

My son has been raised as a vegan. He has never known another way. He does, however, know that the vast majority of people do not live like us. We've always been mindful about not attaching anything "extra" to this fact, allowing him to analyze and understand the eating of animals through his own processes but being there for him for discussion. There are people he loves – his grandmother, a good number of his friends, all of his relatives – who do not look at our place in the world the same way we do and he accepts that he's different, we're different. My son has never minded this all that much and he has always embraced and been proud of his identity as a vegan. I think, though, because it is something that he has always been, he hasn't spent a lot of time thinking about how it might feel to those who are born to be consumed, the actual lives they have. He understands, of course, that animals are killed for food but until he saw those scenes in the movie, I think it was mostly conceptual. Seeing the animals abused with his own eyes, though, made the cruelty very real to my son and his friend. Their suffering was inescapably concrete, no longer just an abstraction.

I recognized something in their faces that afternoon as the three of us talked about their thoughts. I recognized that feeling of knowing that they had seen something that will alter their perspective forever. There is a loss of innocence with that, this knowing that you cannot go back and "unsee" but there is great freedom with it, too. There is a liberation we gain from being allowed the unfiltered truth. In them, I also recognized the same feeling of being stupefied by the business-as-usual approach to the life-and-death matters of animal agriculture as well as the purifying fire that seeing a clear, inexcusable injustice sparks within us. After ten years of being vegan, I saw my son deeply internalize his values on his own terms. He had always happily embraced veganism but seeing what he saw crystallized it for him in a new way.

The next day, our group went to an animal sanctuary near Madison. The kids held roosters, petted pigs, fed goats and helped to clean and prepare the space for a summer camp. They were able to enjoy themselves in a setting far removed from their usual urban lives. The kids were excited to see the animals but felt sadness knowing how few actually manage to find true sanctuary. This is a sane, emotionally intelligent response to exploitation: if you don't feel sad for the other beings that are suffering immensely, you have turned something off. These kids are not conditioned; they are not indoctrinated. It's the opposite. Their heads, and their hearts, are wide open.

We live in a deeply and unnecessarily violent world. Outrage and rebellion against systemic injustice is a terrific and reassuring response. Thank goodness for the people who cry out when others get cut down: they are our hope for the future.

WHEN VEGANS (ALMOST) RULE THE WORLD

I Killed Kale: A Love Story
Originally posted on Thursday, December 8, 2011

What if kale were as idealized by vegans as backyard chickens are by locavores?

What if the leafy greens conferred nobility, honor and a sense of purpose about us as much as the Michael Pollan's elite crowd derives from eating their "special" dairy, eggs, and meat?

This piece was inspired by those who pursue spiritual enlightenment through another being's death, those who cherry pick ephemeral Native American sentiments when they are of benefit to them. After reading a disturbing article by a journalist who traumatizes her children regularly (while patting herself on the back for her good liberal values, of course) by having them watch animals get slaughtered for their table, and yet another website dedicated to the life-and-death cycle of a flock of backyard chickens, I wondered what it might sound like if someone growing kale employed the same hackneyed, self-aggrandizing and narcissistic language and mentality.

This is what I came up with in response.

It seems unbelievable that this life-force a few feet in front of me, past its prime but still standing proud and tall in my garden on this gray early December day, came to me as improbably tiny seeds delivered to my home. As dark brown miniature pebbles, smooth to the touch, these seeds would have been easily dwarfed by the average peppercorn. I held the seeds, little pipsqueaks rolling around in my palm, almost slipping between my fingers, when they arrived in the mail one happy day a few weeks after I'd outlined their picture in a catalogue with a heart, and I beamed with a mother's pride. "They're perfect," I thought, clutching them close to my chest. The delicate seeds held within them the promise that they might eventually blossom into full-grown, hearty and vibrant kale plants that would stretch toward the sun, and after glimpsing their cousins in the catalogue, I immediately knew that I was meant to have them in my own yard.

Over the years, my husband has seen me dive into projects with great gusto only to abandon them within a week or two, so he was understandably skeptical of my plans to take this on and apprehensive about giving over a significant part of our yard, valuable feet to urban dwellers, to any new lark of mine. In my attempts to become more self-reliant, though, I began to reject the idea of buying kale from the grocery store: denatured, limp and lifeless, grown by strangers in unknown conditions (were they overcrowded? Sprayed with chemicals?), plucked from the earth too soon and shipped from far away. I preferred to buy it at the local farmers market, but even with that, I began thinking that I didn't want to ask anyone to do something I wasn't willing to do myself.

I started the tiny seeds indoors in early spring: poking my finger into the soil, I let a few tumble into each hole, then gently covered them back up, like tucking them into bed. I reviewed the instructions on the seed packet daily as though it was my lifeline to them; I watered them enough but not too much, turned them to face the sun equally, kept them warm overnight. I checked on them whenever I thought of it, which was often, scrutinizing the soil many times every day for any signs of life.

One bright Saturday morning, it happened. I woke up and saw that skinny green sprouts had sprung up overnight, right on target with when the packet said that they should. I did a little happy dance and went racing through the house, waking up my husband and son. The sprouts were tiny and fragile but they were the first indisputable evidence of my diligent care. I could do this! These sprouts would eventually grow up into big, bushy plants. At the moment, though, their future was the last thing on my mind. I was just so enamored of these tender little babies, especially proud as they began to mature into hardier seedlings. I showed off their pictures to the friends who indulged me. I sang to the seedlings, gently caressed the soft leaves between my fingers, and every day they seemed to get farther and farther from the little dependent sprouts they'd started out as just a short time ago. They were thriving – heck, they were born - because of me.

When it was time to put them in the garden, I was anxious. The seedlings had been so nurtured and protected in the sunroom of our home. Couldn't springtime's violent windstorms break their delicate stems? What about marauding squirrels, mean birds that might yank them out of the earth just for the sport of it? I fretted over them, so vulnerable out in the elements. I knew, though, that I had to let the seedlings out on their own in the sun, fresh air and soil as nature intended or else they would get strangled by their own roots. As much as I worried about them, my husband gently reminded me to stop being so attached, that these plants were eventually for eating. I tried to ignore him as I planted them outside to flourish.

Flourish they did. The plants seemed to grow taller and more mature, more into their own, by the hour. After just two weeks outdoors, they were clearly no longer wispy little seedlings: they were fully realized plants now, beginning to grow tall and luxuriate in their sheer kaleness. These plants, hand-raised from seeds, were now the essence of healthy kale. It made me choke up whenever I thought of their cousins, raised in unnatural pseudo-farms, stacked one on top of the next in boxes on the produce truck and transported to far-flung destinations. My thriving, beautiful plants were in direct defiance to that sickening approach to vegetable husbandry.

That spring through fall, we enjoyed the chlorophyll-packed leaves we clipped off the mother plant: shredded as salads, in our breakfast scrambles. The kale seemed to grow heartier and bushier with every clipping. Our son was proud of the plants, eager to show them off to friends and to collect leaves for our meals. We planted so many – too many, probably – and they took over more of our yard than we planned. Even my husband didn't mind, though. Looking out into the garden, seeing their happy leaves swaying in the breeze, basking in the gentle early summer's sunshine and gulping the cooling rains of autumn, we knew that we were doing the right thing. The natural thing.

It had become clear by mid-November, though, that the kale plants lived their full life cycle. The leaves, once so full and crisp, were spotted with holes and barely hanging on. There were so many bare spots now, the plants so vulnerable to autumn's deepening winds, and they swayed so intensely with them I thought they might snap right in half. They held on, though it was becoming clear that I would need to assist them on their passage in order to ready the yard for the new life of next spring. This was the natural order, I told myself. They had lived good, complete lives, reveling in their essential kaleness.

It was time. In my heart, I knew that it would eventually come to this.

They had to die.

I steeled myself for the inevitable. They had given me and my family nourishment for months and now it was time for them to die a dignified death befitting such noble leafy greens. My son tried to dissuade me, tearfully asking if we couldn't just bring them indoors for the winter. I repeated the mantra of what we had been talking about all summer: that living under the sky, their roots deep in the earth, was the natural life for kale. Living inside, they would have a shadow of their lives outdoors - austere, constrained, hermetic - far removed from their wild nature. We could keep them alive, but at what cost? His face wet with tears, my son reluctantly nodded, identifying with his child's mind how it feels to be a hemmed in rugged spirit, but he looked away, unable to look at me. I cried, too. Part of his innocence was lost.

Still, he wanted to be there when the kale inhaled its last bit of carbon dioxide. I wanted him there, too, to bear witness and so he could appreciate the life and death cycle that happened in our own back yard. My husband offered to sever the plants, to cut them from their lifeblood, the roots, but I insisted on seeing it through to the end. I was the one, after all, who had raised them from seed, who sang to them as seedlings, caressed them, admired them, watered them, plucked their mature leaves. Looking at them every day, I was filled with gratitude that I was able to give them this life and they in return gave us sustenance and me a sense of connection to the earth, a rootedness I had never felt before. No, I told my husband, I had to see this through from beginning to end for my own spiritual growth.

I took the knife that I knew would do the job the quickest and with a shaky hand, I held the plants once more, pulling them to me, and once again, they yielded to my touch, trusting. Why shouldn't they? All they had ever known was gentleness and care. With a hand shaking so much I didn't know if I could do the job, tears streaming down my face, I took a hiccuping deep breath. They trust you, a voice chided me from inside my head. How could you do this? I am doing it because I love them, I finally responded. With that, I pulled the knife across my first plant.

I can't say that it was easier than I thought it would be. It was harder to cut through than I'd anticipated, gorier. They were once so alive and seconds later, they slumped to the ground, lifeless. No more vitality. My son gasped and sobbed into my husband's chest. One after the next, the kale fell - flump - their roots exposed, their leaves, once so voluptuous, now dry and brittle with age. We stood over them for a few minutes, no one sure what to say, and then we silently began gathering them to take indoors. We would enjoy one last gift from our babies.

That night, we had kale salad, lovingly massaged with olive oil and seasoned just so, and we had a stew, full of their earthy, sweet nutrients. I set aside the stems to use in a stock that will keep nourishing us through the winter. The night of their death, we talked about our favorite memories, the first time they peeped out of the soil, the jaunty seedlings, the early leaves of spring, the powerful plants of autumn. We talked about how we covered them during the big hailstorm of June and we laughed as we remembered how I chased the squirrels away from them all summer.

After dinner, we looked at pictures of them in all their bright verdant glory of early fall. Seeing them like that, my son and I sniffled a bit again, but we knew that our bodies were full of their natural goodness, fed by the sun and the rain and the ebb-and-flow of the seasons. Their death gave us life.

As I tucked my son into bed, we gave thanks again for the kale. Right after turning off the lights, he called me back into his room.

"Yes?" I asked.

"Mom," he asked, his voice in the darkness of his bedroom, "could we grow more kale again in the spring?"

"Of course, my love."

Of course.

End-of-the-line Raw Kale Salad

1 bunch lacinto (dinosaur) kale, shredded and spines removed

½ tablespoon extra virgin olive oil

In a medium bowl, massage the kale and the olive oil between your fingers until the kale softens significantly, about three to four minutes long.

1 tablespoon nutritional yeast

1 teaspoon tamari

1 - 2 teaspoons lemon juice or vinegar of preference

1/8 teaspoon cayenne (opt.)

Salt and freshly ground black pepper to taste

Add the rest of the ingredients to the kale and toss to mix. Very good with toasted, chopped cashews.

WHEN VEGANS (ALMOST) RULE THE WORLD

On Anger and Grief
Originally posted on Wednesday, March 17, 2010

Back when I first came into this life, not my actual birth but my
life as a vegan activist, I immersed myself in learning about the
various ways in which people torture and kill all those beings
unfortunate enough to not have been born in human form. I had
to learn about vivisection, of course, in fact, it was the first thing
I learned about after becoming a vegetarian by way of a poster
up in my school's art building. Just down the pipeline, there was
dog-fighting and puppy mills, circuses and zoos. Oh, and then
rodeos, horse carriages, canned hunts, petting zoos. There was
also that monumental wall I slammed into when I tried to grasp
the enormity of factory farming. I read pamphlet after article after
book, watched videos until I wanted to remove my own horrified
eyes with a grapefruit spoon. Every week, more videos would
arrive in the mail. I watched undercover footage of elephant
abuse that disturbed me so profoundly - John turned off the TV
when I sobbed on the floor more gutturally than either of us ever
knew possible - and I truly believe I have Post-Traumatic Stress
Disorder from seeing it, a part of my innocence permanently
removed like an appendix. I told myself that if the animals had
to endure these traumas, I could at least learn about them, bear
witness to them, speak about them. Anything that I went through
in the process was nothing compared to what they faced.

All around my work office, there were petitions I chased down
my coworkers to sign, postcards about the upcoming anti-fur
march, assertive buttons in a little silver bowl, books and DVDs
lining my shelves, waiting to be lent out. I commandeered the
office printer and ran that thing until my corneas felt like they
would pop out of my head. I went to meeting after meeting in
dark church basements, protest after protest until everything ran
together like a single muddy watercolor. My total immersion into

the world of brutality against animals understandably threatened my natural optimism. The more I read and saw and protested, the angrier I became. How could people be so stupid, so vain, so selfish? This phase of being very angry about the world didn't last long, maybe a year at most: I find people to be just too interesting to shut them out completely. Plus, the person I was becoming just wasn't me. When I emerged from under this dark cloud, I left my preoccupation behind. I decided that unless I was going to run off and join a separatist vegan commune, for the sake of my sanity and quality of life, I could no longer fill my mind with devastating statistics and a steady diet of so much tragic knowledge. Totally steeping in the misery others create was wrecking my life and counter-productive to me being able to attract more people to cruelty-free living. I still value my knowledge and, yes, my outrage, but I just can't pickle myself in it any longer.

Last week I got a taste of it again after a long time away. I was doing research for an article I'm writing about the fur industry. I felt it burbling up again as I held my hand over the gruesome pictures of bloody, skinned corpses, read about a thousand stomach-clenching paragraphs. That familiar cloud rose again. I felt myself mentally spreading cement between bricks, choking out the rest of the world again. I had the benefit of perspective this time, though. I noticed what was happening and I was able to get a grip. Having the good sense to throw out a few lifelines to my compassionate friends helped quite a lot. At times, it was almost as though I were observing someone else go through it. I am able to see now that this rage people accuse animal advocates of having is real: many of us are incredibly angry and justifiably so. Scratch the surface of that white-hot anger, though, and I bet you more times than not, it is there in order to hold back the ocean of sorrow and grief that threatens to sweep us away. Being angry means that you are still alive, you are still fighting, your fuming little heart is still pumping. Being acutely sad means that you feel as if you swallowed a rain cloud and you are slowly drowning internally. Immersing myself again in the world of violence, that was how I felt: like I was slowly drowning.

This all leads me to a great quote I read last week, the one that really helped to pull me out of the sticky morass. (Sometimes those inspiring quotes really do have legs.) This is from Wayne Dyer: "Everything you are against weakens you. Everything you are for empowers you." I read it and my spirit felt lighter, the wisdom of those words trickled through me and for the first time in days, I smiled again. I released my grip on the pain and the anger I'd been lugging around (because I felt like I needed them, I needed something to hold onto) and I noticed that the sun was out, that the squirrel who visits daily was on our back porch again. Sometimes it's intoxicating, that righteous rage, that forceful rejection: it can be energizing and make you feel all tingly. But it's fleeting and when you are just running on the fumes of it, you feel depleted, lost, hopeless, totally isolated in an increasingly hostile, stupid world. Anger is a step up from depression because it can be motivating and bring some fire back into you. Anger is a natural, utterly sane response to this unhinged world. It simply is. Using that anger, though, as a springboard to catapult me toward the life I want to create - rather than toward the ugliness I abhor so I can continue to fruitlessly pummel my fists against it - is the objective. When I am inspired by and grounded in the passion for what I love, I have endless vitality, the creative flow is so undeniably moving, the pieces just seem to snap into place so effortlessly. Comparing this to when I am solely fueled by anger: well, when I am moving toward and inspired by what I am for, I am in the driver's seat rather than just a passenger. It becomes a reciprocal relationship then, rather than one-sided, when I am both feeding and actually being nourished by the things in life that inspire me. I think this is true for all of us.

What a relief it is to throw off the burden of this pain and to know that dwelling in it is simply not necessary. This releasing of the grief and anger doesn't make us less compassionate, less

knowledgeable, less concerned: I think that sometimes we hold
onto it because we don't know who we'd be without it, like
we'll fly away like dry leaves. In truth, when you move towards
what you are for rather than what you are against, you have
permission to be wildly, passionately but peacefully you. Living
as an example of someone who is moving toward and motivated
by what she loves is incredibly inspiring and liberating to others.
And this is what is going to change the world.

WHEN VEGANS (ALMOST) RULE THE WORLD

When Vegans Attack!

Originally posted on Thursday, August 2, 2012

Officers of law ticket civilians, they sneak up on us, they maintain the rules and order but, most important for my purposes here, the police have also taken a solemn oath to be sworn Enemies of Fun. As someone who gets that sinking feeling whenever I spot a police car behind my own, I share that visceral negative reaction people have with officers: Oh, no! I wish they weren't right behind me. Oh, damn, I hope I don't get pulled over for anything. Are all my city stickers up-to-date? Can't they just turn off and go somewhere else? A police officer showing up while people are just safely minding their own business creates a universal "wah wah waaaah" sound effect that is part of our shared experience. We all feel suddenly and conspicuously guilty in the presence of a police officer.

Vegans, just by our mere existence, can have a similar affect it seems. As a result, our presence creates resentment and agitation, whether we are outspoken advocates or not, simply because of what we represent. A vegan at a barbecue is the equivalent of a nun at an orgy: the buzz-kill, the drag, the spoilsport. If only we weren't around, there would be one bacchanal of a feast – bacon hanging from the rafters, oozy cheese flowing out of every spout, a small mountain of hot, battered and deep-fried animal parts on every countertop – but, no, we had to show up and be all vegan about it, making everyone else feel bad with our sour faces. Why can't omnivores just enjoy life without us prudes always showing up and managing to ruin their good time?

I was sort of accused of being aligned with "the vegan police" not too long ago. I had expressed unhappiness with a certain famous author, one who had written a well-regarded book that looked at the ethical implications of eating animals, but who, a couple of years later, started promoting more "humane" ways of eating them. This was disappointing and simply sad to me: why create all these new labels (often meaningless) and standards (often toothless) when the bottom line is that eating animals is unnecessary and necessarily exploitative and cruel? Why must we devise labyrinthine, opaque systems for avoiding the inevitability that taking another's life for a momentary pleasure is simply unjustifiable? There are few wrongs in life that are so lacking in nuance and also so easily rectified than this one. A friend disagreed with my perspective and characterized what I'd said as being reminiscent of "the vegan police." I was a little offended, sure, but more than that, it got me thinking about the meaning of this term.

Those accused of being vegan police are the humorless, severe and ultra-orthodox arbiters of good and evil. We measure life by a certain moral yardstick and we are always on the right side of that yardstick. We are busybodies, preoccupied with patrolling others. When the vegan police walk into the room, all merriment ceases, the dancing ladies stop doing the can-can, the piano player freezes over his keys and you could hear a pin drop until, like lightning, all the fun quickly bolts out the nearest doors and windows.

I have to say that I get it.

Even as a member by default of this particular order, there are some vegans I am nervous of making a perceived mistake in front of – and not a "mistake" like, say, eating chicken, but a mistake like voicing support for the "wrong" organization. We walk that moral razor's edge daily, and we can easily lose our footing and go teetering in either direction depending on how our lives are interpreted by others. Activists wield emotionally charged terms (for example, the always-in-vogue abolitionist vs. welfarist polarity) as if they were cudgels, and, in turn, many of us shrink into ourselves, afraid to reveal anything that could paint us with a label that diminishes us. In our efforts to hold ourselves and each other up to impeccable standards, we can become neurotic and tyrannical hard-liners. I've seen this dynamic of shaming and one-upmanship, as well as the chilling effect it creates, too many times to deny its presence in the vegan community.

We should voice our differing views, though, because we need to be honest. To be intimidated into silence or cajoled into towing the party line of solidarity is a very damaging approach, one far too reminiscent of a twisted family dynamic for me to participate in. I believe that while we do nitpick one another to death sometimes, arguing over this or that fine point when our core values are aligned, it doesn't mean that we shouldn't openly disagree with one another, sometimes vigorously so. The social justice movement that we are actively creating together is something novel and audacious and shot through with ambition. It is also unprecedented. There is no question that we are going to argue and disagree as we find our way through this work and that is the only honest way to do it. Despite how it is often depicted, veganism isn't a cult. We have no position papers. Creating a social justice movement for those whose exploitation is so deeply entrenched throughout the world – with all people, regardless of wealth or social status, taking advantage - is hugely difficult, messy work. We need to hash this out and accept that we won't necessarily always or even often agree. We just need one component, though, that seems to be in short supply.

The essential piece of the equation is respect.

Why do we jump to the worst conclusions about one another? Why do we rush to judgement? Why are vegans our own worst enemies? Time and time again, I have seen good people vituperated during disagreements, treated as if they were just one small step above the worst animal abusers themselves. Why? Why the lack of nuance and inability to see the big picture? Is it because social media, where so much of this plays out, lacks the painful consequences of real life and reinforces those with poor impulse control? Is it just a symptom of living in a violent world, one that we can't help but let influence our interactions?

I suspect that there are multiple causes. We need to understand this better. In the meantime, though, we can all try to not see the very worst in one another. We are a tiny minority and face a monolithic, uphill struggle as we try to change how society functions on the most far-reaching and altruistic level history has seen. Make no mistake, the vegan movement is made of boldness. Feelings will be hurt. I'm not asking for a group hug or a drum circle or even for us to share our best source for affordable yet stylish vegan shoes with one another. Not at all. We won't always get along but we could perhaps give each other a break once in a while, right? We could give one another the benefit of the doubt occasionally, even when our fingers are dying to tell someone off and smack that return key, couldn't we? Could we show one another the empathy, compassion and tenderness we regularly feel for battery chickens? I think it shouldn't be that hard.

Remember that while we are condemning and berating one another, people who are just beginning to explore veganism are looking on. Is that what we want to show them, that their new community will seize upon any perceived mistake they make, be it linguistic, tactical or just a difference of opinion? That is no way to grow a movement and, damn it, we need one another and many, many more of us if we are going to make this thing work in a meaningful way.

So here are some quick things you can do instead of flying off the handle at a Very, Very Wrong Vegan. You can:

Take a deep breath. (In with peace, out with anger…In with peace, out with anger…)

Punch a pillow.

Take a cardio-boxing class.

Spend an hour playing with kittens at an animal shelter.

Read some Sylvia Plath.

Watch reality TV and scream at your television until you feel all better.

Do what you need to do to get the mean reds out of your system and then come up for air again. When you can speak honestly but not abusively, you are in a good place to create a dialogue. This is only common sense but sometimes we all need reminders.

There is too much at stake for us to self-destruct. Let's do this thing.

Girl Bully

Originally posted on Tuesday, November 3, 2009

Imagine this eleven-year-old girl with a crazy, black mushroom cloud for hair - it was a poorly executed Dorothy Hamill "wedge," earning about a 1.2 score by the judges simply for the effort – during the preppy era, surrounded by straight-haired blondes who all seemed to be at least a foot taller than her. In sixth grade, that was me. Oh, I also had boobs. This was the year that my elementary school joined three or four others, all tributaries feeding into one violently fast-flowing, bubbling river of hormones and anxieties that was our collective junior high. My inner-life, never exactly placid, was especially tumultuous at this time. Whenever my father was home, he was either on a rampage or, blessedly, passed out cold; my mother wandered our tidy suburban house with perpetually red-rimmed eyes from crying, lines deepening on her forehead and I was petrified that she'd die of grief and leave us with Him. My sixth grade homeroom teacher was a notorious bully and a certifiable jackass. My next-door neighbor and best friend's father – a truly gracious, heroic man who I often imagined was my own father – died of leukemia the winter I was in sixth grade. Many of my old friends, girls I'd played with since I was in kindergarten, suddenly became nervous with the influx of new kids with better hair and froze me out. It was an awful time.

Add just one more external stress to everything else that was dreadful: an incredibly mean-spirited school bully who had me, the girl with the mushroom cloud for hair, in her sights. It is easy to see why I was singled out and it was pretty much a numbers game anyway: each of us except for the upper echelon of popular kids had a tormentor of some variety and she just happened to be my personal bully. There were others in line behind her to pick up the slack when necessary, for sure, mean boys and their female counterparts who would snicker and shove and say cruel things just to inflict harm pretty much daily. If there was a day that was without much taunting – the mean kids had to refuel occasionally and restock their munitions – where I could get from Point A to Point B with a minimum of viciousness directed at me, I was floating on the clouds, that was such a joyous day. It was a rare occurrence and usually just a matter of sheer luck when this girl, let's call her The Wench for clarity's sake, didn't seize on me like a heat-seeking missile.

The Wench had gone to one of the other elementary schools: she was tall and skinny with a large, crooked nose and a witch-y, long face (or perhaps my judgment is clouding my memory). She was athletic and was befriended by The Right People, Nordic-looking girls and sporty boys, probably way back in kindergarten or first grade. Thankfully we never had homeroom together, but when we passed in the hall, or in gym class or lunch, I was fair game. "Nice hair," The Wench would say, screwing up her mouth into a sneer. "You are so pretty!" Or, "Hey, can you teach me how to be just like you? You're so awesome." Day in and day out, The Wench was on my trail. She would pretend that popular boys liked me, that I was invited to parties I knew I wasn't, that I was every bit as awesome as she knew herself and her feathered-hair friends to be. Right before she'd say something new, The Wench would squint her already beady black eyes at me, smirk and reach into her inner bag of tricks for some more ammunition, or she would look me down from head-to-toe and just riff off whatever she felt inspired by - my clothes, my hair, my being - like some highly talented jazz artist of misanthropy. My stomach hurt pretty much every day of school in sixth and seventh grade; whenever I'd walk in those front doors, a deep sense of dread would sink inside me like an anchor. Kerplunk. By eighth grade, The Wench had other fixations (boys) and largely left me alone as I recall. I was in the throes of anorexia by then, shrinking ultimately to 75 pounds and growing hair on my concave belly, so I was quite literally in the process of disappearing. By the next year, high school, I had beat anorexia and was able to get lost in the sea of others. The Wench became insignificant at our complexly tiered high school, no longer ruling the hallways and the cafeteria with her cackling understudies, and she, too, got lost in the sea of people. After junior high, our paths rarely crossed.

Last week, though, lo and behold, I got a "friend request" from The Wench via my Facebook account. My first thought, after my eyeballs pretty much jumped out of my head and I breathed into a paper bag for a few minutes, was, "Oh, she's making fun of me again? She still thinks that I am going to fall for that one?" My next thought was, "How dare you?"

I know that growing up we all face untold indignities and attacks against our pride. I know that I was not alone, nor was I necessarily singled out much more than the average dorky kid at my school. But I also know how very painful that time in my life was, how I wished that I could just fade away and disappear when she (or one of the others) had me in her sights. They were so darn effective at what they did, in fact, that they made me want disappear altogether, not just when they were near. We tend to minimize childhood cruelties when we grow up: oh, it wasn't that bad. I survived. Or we ponder that perhaps our bullies had bad home lives. To that I say, yes, I survived (is mere survival what we're striving for in life?) and, yes, it was that bad. When we're children, especially those of us in an unsupportive home environment, that is our reality and as our life experiences are so limited, it is very difficult for such bullying to be anything but hugely painful. And maybe she did have a bad home life. You know what? So did I, a really awful one. She made a horrible time in my life just that much worse.

I went on from that wretched junior high to high school and then to college, finally meeting the sort of people who made me feel good about who I was, who supported me as I discovered who I was after so many years of being defined by others. By the time I graduated college, I was confident, happy and assertive:

my friends from around this time couldn't believe that there'd ever been a time when I was cowering by my locker, hoping beyond hope that someone like The Wench wouldn't spot me as she did her daily sweep of the hall. I emerged from the cocoon I'd built for myself apprehensively but with determination: I would never be vulnerable to a hateful bully again.

I briefly – like for less than a second – contemplated accepting her friend request if just so she could see that I survived her beautifully, that I have a great life and fantastic friends. But then I realized I didn't want The Wench to have access to my life on any level. She already took too big a bite out of it. Even by the loose definition of "friend" that seems to be Facebook's operating description – that a "friend" is someone you know, or someone your friends know – The Wench doesn't count as a friend of mine. Friendship is too sacred to me. Friends are those who want the best for you in their hearts. Friends are those who make your heart lighten up just a little to think about. Friends are there for you when you are at your most vulnerable and they never, ever exploit that or get a cheap thrill out of making you hurt worse.

My finger hit the "ignore" button (oh, how I wish that said something else, more like, "Denied!" or "Screw you!") and it felt astonishingly good.

Oh. And fuck off, Wench.

On Gratitude

Originally posted on Tuesday, November 24, 2009

The Body

Today I am grateful that I don't have a sprained ankle, a migraine or a weird, darting pain in my back. I am grateful for limbs that work as my brain signals for them to do, for joints that move painlessly and even for that scar on my wrist because it reminds me of roller-skating down a hill in the summer and because it's a good story. I am not grateful for the pimple between my eyes, but I am grateful that there are no others and that it is on its downward descent. I'm grateful that my eyes can blink on their own, I can swallow without help from a medical device, that my days are uninterrupted by pain or a million little aches or beeping machines hooked up to my arms. I am grateful for this strong, able body, and that I can brace myself and slice through the Chicago winds without being tossed around like a dirty plastic bag, getting myself caught in bare tree branches. I am grateful that I can slip on ice and not fear of breaking my hip; I can do a head-to-toe analysis as I look up at the puffy clouds overhead from the sidewalk and know with a relative certainty that nothing is broken. I am grateful for these two strong hands that stir batter until it all comes together and looks just right and for fingers that hit letter after letter on the keyboard, but that can also be gentle, for wiping my son's tears, for touching a cheek, for entwining my fingers in another's. I'm grateful for all this and more.

The Things

Today I am grateful that I can turn a handle and water pours forth, that it is predictably there and without strange little minnows swimming in circles in it as was the case in my childhood anxieties. I am grateful for this computer that gets cursed at a lot but has been the vehicle for keeping me in touch

127

with people near oceans and in deserts, for reconnecting me with childhood friends I thought I'd lost forever, for meeting people I may never see face-to-face but who inspire me daily, for being instrumental to hatching plans and firming thoughts and giving birth to ideas. I am grateful for my orange-yellow, glittery bike, and my two strong legs that propel me forward, for being the vehicle as I push through space with my own body as the motor, passing the cars as they idle at the stoplight. I am grateful for glass windows that keep out the cold and for oscillating fans when the winter seems as distant as a shadowy dream and for tea, year-round. I am grateful for doors I can lock and that there's no one in my life whom I'd like to lock out again. I am grateful for our pink and orange rooms, for the dining room wall full of pictures, for all those books with dog-eared pages and the old-fashioned radiators we fill with water when it finally gets so dry that we remember. I am grateful for our bathroom, though it's nothing fancy, and for the smooth wooden floor under our feet. I'm grateful for all this and more. (Let's not forget dark chocolate and Satsuma mandarin oranges and hot peppers.)

The Feelings

Today I am grateful for the many glass jars of spices that make me feel like a magician when I cook, a pinch of this, a teaspoon of that, my feet dancing back and forth with self-assurance, and for feeling when I do this that I'm reconnecting with a piece of my grandmother's sweet spirit. I am grateful for making people laugh, for those who see me at my worst but don't turn away, for the way my heart does a little dance when my son tells me he loves me, so pure and unguarded. I am grateful for more good days than bad, for moods that seem more level, for being more certain that I'm here for a reason, and for each day when I can feel this buzzing inside like a million bumblebees. I'm grateful for purposefulness and for silliness, and for any time I can calibrate the perfect balance of both. I am grateful for the love I feel, for the flame of hope that can't be extinguished despite all common sense sometimes, for the way I feel when I do more or better or more generously than I expected. I am grateful for making strangers smile – or even laugh, an uncommon treat – for the way I feel when the birds start singing in the spring (full of hope and anticipation and deep inhalations, that's all I can say) and for the way I felt when my grandfather looked at me, his eyes full of love. I am grateful that he taught me how one can convey more in a simple glance than a thousand words, even though that hasn't stopped me from trying. I am grateful for that little girl who never believed for a second that she was inferior to a boy and who grew up to be me. I am grateful that I live in a time and a place when I can live according to my values and desires rather than something imposed on me. I'm grateful for all this and more.

The Others

Today I am grateful for the many people who make me laugh and smile and actively savor living in the moment. I am grateful for the four-legged companions I've been blessed to share a home with, for what they've taught me about enjoying life with all they've got. I am grateful for Lenny, my dearly departed dog and hound-shaped soul mate, who looked at me with those soft eyes of pure, uncomplicated love (exactly the way my grandfather looked at me) on the last day of his life, wagging his tail just to see me even when we both knew death was so close. I am grateful for our cat and her little black button nose, perfect little thing, and for the way I feel when I see her looking out the front window as I'm coming home. I am grateful for all the wise and hilarious and deeply human friends of mine who try so hard not to accept the ordinary and challenge me to be my best, too. I am grateful for my son, who lets me know when I'm being mean or impatient, who teaches me so much about loving who one is as is, who thinks I should have my own bakery I'm that good. I am grateful that he teaches me to love without condition because I can be such a jerk sometimes. I am grateful for my mother and her big, kind heart, who gets teary when she sees a total stranger cry, who is so profoundly unmaterialistic she cannot receive a compliment without offering the object to the admirer.

129

I am grateful for my aunt, who loves her sister fiercely and for loving me when I was a child as if I were her own. I am grateful for my brother, who has never let our different natures put a wedge between us. I am grateful for all the animals I have met at shelters and sanctuaries, who have taught me to keep shining my light no matter what, who are deeply resilient and full of innate dignity. I am grateful for John, for too much to say here, for too many things but here's a start: for the big smile, for trying to make me laugh when I'm in a snit, for his compassion and grace, for always wanting the best for me (how many can honestly say this?), for his mind that never stops, for his boundless curiosity, for his inability to conceal it when he thinks something is really fantastic, for thinking that I'm fantastic, for teaching me that I am worthy of love by such a good-hearted person. I'm grateful for all this and more.

Thanks to all who have made mine such a lovely life. I am truly grateful for it.

The Next Emancipation

Originally posted on Thursday, December 6, 2012

Over the weekend, we saw *Lincoln*. I am always embarrassed by how little I know of this critical time in U.S. history, so shot through with upheaval. After seeing the film, I was especially struck by the character of Thaddeus Stevens, someone I knew nothing about, played with a fiery but believable zeal by Tommy Lee Jones.

Thaddeus Stevens was chairman of the powerful House Ways and Means committee and a key Radical Republican; by all accounts, he was consumed with such a profound and visceral contempt for slavery, roiled by the thought of it, that he made it his life's work to eradicate it. Today, it's easy to take an emphatic moral position against slavery: is there even any reasonable counter-argument? In the 1860s, though, with much of the country in ruins, no end in sight to the horrific combat and hundreds of thousands of deaths already tallied, it was not such an easy political stance, nor was racial equality considered a given. This was a pivotal time in American history, one where the United States could have easily fissured, but President Lincoln and Thaddeus Stevens (among others) remained deeply committed to getting the 13th Amendment ratified on the Constitution.

Imagine the pressure. Imagine the misgivings. Imagine the nights of sleepless anguish.

There were many times in watching the film that I saw clear parallels to the uphill battle vegan activists face in our struggle to have 98% of the population consider the rights of others on moral grounds. There seem to be some obvious similarities to the obstacles abolitionists faced. For example, those who wanted to maintain the status quo depicted the anti-slavery campaigners

131

as ridiculous, dangerous and worse. White people were born with the right to own slaves as part of their natural prerogative, after all, ordained by God. (Even many of those who didn't keep slaves still didn't want to believe that slaves were as human as they were.) Similarly, vegan advocates are often characterized as ridiculous, dangerous and worse by those who want to maintain the status quo of animal exploitation and use. Further, people of faith and atheists alike consider that it's a given that animals are ours to eat and use as we see fit. Whether they say that this was what God decreed or they say, well, sorry but that's the way things are (in so many words), the bottom line is the same: the animals are ours and we have every right to them. Interestingly, some justifications were also similar, for example, the attitude among anti-abolitionists that they were doing it for the good of the slaves, a kind of benevolence: what would all those feeble-minded slaves do if they were suddenly freed? They would not be able to fend for themselves, to feed themselves. Today, we hear the same flawed rationalization for maintaining animal agriculture. If we no longer killed animals for food, they would not only overwhelm our resources and land, they wouldn't be able to care for themselves.

I am not one who likes to compare historic or contemporary tragedies to each other and say that one is the equivalent of the other. I believe that this cheapens the suffering and diminishes the individuality of those who have been oppressed. When a sentient being is in anguish, the suffering is uniquely experienced by that individual. For this reason, I don't like saying what the animals experience is like slavery or the Holocaust. This is not because "they're just animals" but because I think that doing so over-simplifies the specific anguish the individuals suffered, whether human or otherwise. I do think that there are parallels, though, with slavery: the concepts of ownership, of sovereignty, of emphasizing the powerful majority's "right" to the entitlements they want to preserve versus the right of those not so endowed to simply live their own lives. In short, the chilling mentality of exceptionalism.

The essential questions we have to ask of ourselves are also eerily similar: Where do we draw the line in regards to another's rights and why do we draw them there? Are the relatively small forfeitures we make in order to end our role in harming another really tantamount to giving up our supposed rights? Is something truly a right or did we inherit it due to existing power structures that unjustly favor us?

The unfair and unnecessary brutality against animals is not going to end unless the world begins to think in moral terms about something as seemingly benign as ordering a chicken salad sandwich. In the 1860s and before, it was considered laughable to think of the lives of the slaves working the field and the moral implications of saying that another being belongs to someone else. Today, we are told the same about the animals people like to eat and exploit. Why? To live with honesty and integrity, there are times when we have to make uncomfortable reckonings with ourselves.

I truly believe that this is our social justice movement of the day. Our blatant and unspoken acceptance of the human domination of other animals is something that the overwhelming majority of people don't want to face. If some comparisons make us feel uncomfortable, though, that may be a signal that it is something to explore. Within this discomfort, we can reveal a painful truth: there are more similarities than differences between the mentality that allows for slavery and the mentality that allows for eating animals than many of us would care to admit.

20 Things I'd Rather Do Than Hear You Go On About Your Paleo Diet

Originally posted on Monday, April 8, 2013

1. Drop a kettlebell on my foot.

2. Get pulled over for speeding with an expired license in a car that has failed the emissions test with a "Bad Cop, No Donut" bumper sticker.

3. Be the sole adult responsible for two dozen 3rd graders at a large waterpark on "free soda refills" day.

4. Learn that the guy sitting next to me on my six-hour airplane ride is an evangelist who also sells timeshares. Plus, he's very chatty.

5. Run into an ex on sweatpants-and-shower-free Sunday.

6. Forget to bring any of my 3,068 canvas bags on the day that the teacher who runs my son's Green Team is behind me in the checkout lane at the grocery store.

7. Notice just a little too late that the expiration date on my coconut yogurt was two weeks ago.

8. Be on a nearly empty train and have the guy who keeps muttering, twitching and scratching himself decide to sit down right next to me.

9. You know that feeling when your car seems a little louder than usual and keeps pulling in one side and you're all like, "Please don't let it be a flat tire," and then you hear that flapping sound so you pull over to check and, indeed, it's flat? I'd rather feel that.

10. Get stuck on an elevator with the guys from #4 and #8. And a small marching band.

11. Walk barefoot over a floor my son has scattered with Legos. (Wait, I already do that.)

12. Mistake the curry powder for the cinnamon on my morning oatmeal.

13. Get on the bus driven by the driver who has decided that today is the day she's going to show the other motorists who's boss.

14. Hear the train approaching as I am putting my money in to get a train card but the machine keeps spitting out my dollar and the train is getting closer and I am desperately trying to flatten out the dollar against the machine but goddamn it! It's not working.

15. That little speck of dust on my dog? It just jumped and, upon closer inspection, there are many, many more of them.

16. Realize that my keys are in my other coat pocket after I've already pulled the locked door shut. And so is my phone.

17. Notice that my parking meter is expired two minutes after the person writing the ticket did.

18. Have someone discreetly whisper to me that my skirt is tucked into my tights at a big event I've organized twenty minutes after I was last in the bathroom. (I speak from experience on this one and I'd still rather have this happen again.)

19. Remember at 10:30 p.m. that we are out of toothpaste.

20. You know how sometimes the bunch of bananas you bought looked fine on the outside but then when you pull down the peel, they're all weird and squishy and rotten inside? Yeah, that. Plus now you have fruit flies.

All this and more, people! How about you?

Serve With Fava Beans and a Nice Chianti: The Hannibal Lecterism of Happy Meat

Originally posted on Tuesday, October 23, 2012

I was originally drawn to her because of the rare quality of her breeding. The moment I saw the young female, I knew that I was the perfect person to be entrusted to see her through to the end.

I had had a young female the year before, a close relative of hers, and her fine heritage took me aback. She spoiled me for life: I couldn't go back to having those of an inferior caliber again. When it was time that I wanted to have another one, I knew I wanted one of her pedigree once more, but I didn't want to just be a passive bystander in her death again. Something within me needed a different experience. This time, I had to actively participate in her death, until her last shudder, and follow that through to her complete disassembly. The entirety of the young female would be used very purposefully and with great intention.

She had been born into a life of high standards. Being a rare creature myself, I recognized this in her. There are too many females of interior genetics, ones who are common and low born, and this one was cut from a different cloth. She was special and lovely and she had to be that way in order for me to consider having her as mine. Of course I wanted to see how she lived so I would have a deeper appreciation of how she was to die.

I wanted her parts, the internal organs, her viscera, the blood of her, still fresh and warm. I wanted her tender flesh, cut from her with my trusted instruments and pulled with my own hands. I wanted to understand the elegant, clever design of her before I consumed her, and I wanted to break her down personally. I wanted to find creative uses for every last inch of her so her life wouldn't have been taken in vain.

Seeing her in out her natural habitat, breathing in the crisp autumn air, I knew that I made the right decision. She wasn't like the others, the poor, pathetic creatures that have been so damaged by poor genetics and circumstances. This one was different. She was a perfect specimen of her variety, a natural female, her pretty cheeks warmed by the sun to a golden peach. This was a young female who had felt gentle breezes blowing through her auburn hair, who had never been mistreated by course, rough hands, who had dined on organic blueberries she'd plucked from a neighbor's garden with her own graceful hands. I insisted that she live no less of a life before I would take it from her.

That day, I spent an hour getting to know her and she seemed to trust me from the start. I rubbed her shoulders, and I touched her hair, warm from the sun. She was playful, affectionate, spirited. She smiled easily, clearly enjoying this life, and she had no idea of my intentions. This began to make me very uneasy but I told myself that it was better this way, better that her life would end with someone she trusted rather than at a stranger's hands in an unfamiliar, cold setting. This was much more humane. Breathing deeply to keep my emotions in check, I held her hands in mine. I looked my young female in the eye. I told her that I was grateful for what she was about to give me. I may have even shed a tear. I have consumed countless young females in my lifetime, but being there then was a deeper, richer experience, though one fraught with tension. I wouldn't have traded it for anything in the world.

In the end, her death was astonishingly quick and easy – two quick bullets – which is fortunate because there was no time to waste.

First I carefully undressed her and then I began collecting my blood. I'd never had this before so it was a priority. I had to make that everything was positioned right to bleed my body properly, otherwise all that good blood would be squandered. It was a struggle propping everything correctly and I questioned whether I was cut out for this work but in the end, I was successful and I am very glad that I had the persistence to see this dream of mine – fresh blood – realized and that I didn't quit.

That task completed, there was a lot of work ahead of me, which meant scalding, scraping, cutting through fat, muscles, tendons, and tugging out organs. As repulsive as it might sound to an outsider, it was a breathtakingly clean and methodical process, breaking down the body bit by bit and seeing how the organs looked and felt close up: the heart, the kidneys, the bladder, one by one, I observed them with the cool-headed precision of a surgeon and gently placed them in my container. The bright pink lungs in particular, lungs that just a short time ago had breathed in the same cool fall air as I, were especially noteworthy. She did not disappoint.

Separating the intestines from the fat and other tissues meant that with just a good cleaning, I now had sausage casing that I had pulled from a body I chose with my own hands and technical skills. It was hard to not feel prideful pulling out handful after handful of healthy intestine. This makes it all worthwhile, I thought to myself as my organ container continued to fill, steam slowly rising from it. The young female was no longer of this world but all these different parts and pieces would extend her life far beyond her reach as a living being. The incredible responsibility I felt of needing to continue to provide stewardship for the young female even after her death was a profound realization.

After she was fully broken down and stored properly, I felt I owed it to myself and to her to finally enjoy the fruits of my labor. Carving bits of her flesh on my butcher block, I was able to quietly to reflect on our symbiotic relationship: she gave her life to provide nourishment for me and I was able to consume her with true appreciation for her fine quality. We gave this to each other.

In a beloved cast iron skillet that once belonged to my grandmother, I sautéed delicately sliced pieces of her flesh with minced garlic, baby carrots, parsnips and fresh purple basil and thyme from my garden. The scent of her filled the air: rich, savory, mouthwateringly alluring. A splash of her blood to thicken the sauté was an inspired improvisation, I think.

Sitting down to finally enjoy the meal I'd created, I knew that I had made the right choice. She was tender but perfectly substantial, sinewy in certain places but nicely balanced by her delicate texture. Her flavor so effectively captured her essence that at times, it was as if she was still with me, sitting across the table from me, her hair glinting in the candlelight. I toasted her spirit.

In all, it was a beautiful, bittersweet experience. I couldn't help ruminating on how she slumped back with that first bullet, the look of shock and horror marring her perfect features along with the spray of blood. I thought of how much work it was to collect all the blood, how exhausted I felt, pulling out the intestines but how I had to do right by this young female. She would live on to be my steaks, sausages, burgers and bacon for the year as well as provide bits for stew, gravy, casings and so on. I think she would be proud to know how very well used she would be.

After this experience, I will never again take another's life and death for granted. When it comes time for me to harvest another young female, I will bring this same intentionality and poignancy. It will be my gift back to those who give me their lives and it is my gift to myself. I will do right by all the future young females who will grace my butcher block. You can count on that.

If you think that this is extreme, please read this first hand account of the slaughter of a pig by popular Chicago butcher, Rob Levitt. <http://m.chicagoreader.com/Bleader/archives/2012/10/17/a-butcher-meets-his-meat> *With me just making one simple, easy switch of who the victim is, suddenly it's evident that the story was written by a psychopath, despite the key details remaining essentially unchanged.*

WHEN VEGANS (ALMOST) RULE THE WORLD

The self-aggrandizement, as well as the perfectly clinical and Hannibal Lecter-esque narrative, were deeply disturbing to me in Rob Levitt's essay. It is one thing to mindlessly eat animals. It is another thing to romanticize the special flesh you consume, to repeat the narcissistic myths you want to think that eating it says about you. Make no mistake, it is the mindless consumption that is creating the immense death toll of ten billion land animals in the U.S. each year, but it is this arrogant, self-serving mentality of entitlement that is so pervasive among Happy Meat enthusiasts that I find deeply chilling. It is also what has me thinking as a satirist.

If my essay was disturbing to you, that is a good thing. It means you can still feel. Thanks to Nicole from Upton's Naturals, a dedicated vegan protein company, for bringing it to my attention.

Global Vegan Domination: The Plan
Wednesday, May 2, 2012

All right, Sally Fallon, Nina Planck and Fox News, you've discovered our secret plan. It's time to stop beating around the bush and time to lay our cards on the table. We are a reasonable people. It's not a big deal. It's just that from every corner of the world, we herbivores are mating and adopting children with the intention of creating an army of cold-eyed vegan spawn who will swat the hot dogs right out of your innocent hands. They won't say a word and that will be the most menacing part of this assault on your civil liberties: they will just get a mean little squint in their eyes and then boom - your hot dog will be on the ground. Omnivore, it doesn't matter if you're clutching fast-food chicken sandwiches or grass-fed beef, conventional dairy or free-range eggs: our child army will find you and that is when you'll realize that acid reflux is the least of your problems. Look around the playground. See that little boy on the swings, the girl in braids hanging from the parallel bars?

They are watching you.

They are not happy.

We are not happy.

Oh, we are so pissed but we have plans. We are so certain that we will be victorious that we're letting you know what our plans are.

First, we will take your jobs. All superiors will also be replaced with one of us. You will be sent packing without a sad little party or even a card. We will fill every staff kitchen and vending machine with flax crackers, dehydrated acai berries and coconut water. This will be our fuel. Doubt us? Who is going to have the stamina, the ability to outrun, climb, dodge and outwit? The omnivores? Good one. And who is going to have the dogged persistence and fortitude necessary for such a bold uprising? Who are the ones who have been told to "eat around" meat, dealt with annoying questions at Thanksgiving and have been the punch line to every single office comedian's joke for-freaking-ever. That's right. It's going to be the vegans. This includes political office, too, in case you were wondering.

Then we're going to move in next door to you. We're going to rip out all the grass and plant every variety of kale we can get our hands on - curly, red, lacinto – so every neighborhood is a sea of leafy greens. We're going to ferment cabbage with the windows open all summer long. And who is that looking over the fence or balcony at you while you're grilling dead animal parts? Why, it's us and our cold-eyed children. We will direct delivery trucks dropping off our weekly supply of nutritional yeast to double-park in front of your car and we will run our high-speed blenders at 6:00 in the morning on weekends just to be mean because that is who we are. Our kids will have green smoothie lemonade stands and teach your kids about the enslavement of so-called food animals. Next, they will cover circuses, rodeos, vivisection. If you think we're bad, you will shudder when you meet our children. They have chlorophyll for blood, an implant that screens Meet Your Meat continuously in their heads and they are unstoppable.

Next, we will take over the schools. The new schedules will look like this:

First period: Sun salutations

Second period: Strategies in total global domination

Third period: Classics in revolutionary literature

Fourth period: Movement theory workshop

Fifth period: Vegan potluck

Sixth period: Omnivorous atrocities through the ages

Seventh period: Vegan rock star chorus

Eighth period: The social science of insurgencies

Our schools will have classroom after classroom filled with cold-eyed vegan children and teenagers raised on tofu scramble and filled with revolutionary zeal. In short, you're screwed.

Finally, we become the media. When Big Vegan takes over, not only will we write and report the news, we will determine all the programming and create the content. Every sitcom, reality show, talk show and drama will be developed from a vegan framework and overtly designed to topple omnivorism. A sample on any given night? **NBC:** A vegan confronts her family about their blatant speciesism on the Kathy Freston Show. **HBO:** Four stylish best friends representing different archetypes navigate the ups-and-downs of the NYC vegan dating scene (Episode 4: Eleanor feels insecure when her boyfriend flirts with the hot young anarchist at the Occupy Omnivorism protest. Should they break up?) **Bravo:** The Real Vegan Power Couples of the Bay Area. You don't like television? We will run all newspapers and radio stations as well. None of this is close to approximating the international arsenal of bloggers we are prepared to unleash, either.

So, as you can see, we will be infiltrating everything. We will be everywhere. We will be the judge when you are contesting a traffic ticket. We will be the parents of the girl you are trying to impress. We will run the neighborhood zoning committee and will be on the board of your condo association. We will be the ones who switched on the police car lights you just noticed in your rear view mirror.

It's best just to submit, omnivore. It's happening.

You can't say we didn't warn you.

About Marla Rose

Marla Rose is a writer, activist and community builder actively involved in Chicago's flourishing vegan movement.

In 1998, she and her husband created the pioneering vegan web magazine, Vegan Street. In 1999, at the request of the "Mad Cowboy" Howard Lyman, Marla co-founded and headed the Chicago chapter of EarthSave International, eventually producing an annual event called *The Conference for Conscious Living* that drew dozens of vegan leaders to Chicago over the next decade. This event ultimately grew into the innovative and popular festival, *Chicago VeganMania*, which has drawn thousands of attendees over the last four years. Meanwhile, Marla co-founded the Chicago Vegan Family Network, which has grown into a group of dozens of families all raising vegan children. In 2009, Marla and her husband were recognized by Mercy For Animals as Activists of the Year.

In 2004, Marla published her first book, *Marla's Vegan Guide to Chicago and the Universe*. Soon after, she began posting on *Vegan Feminist Agitator*, which has been the basis for this book. She is a regular feature writer for *VegNews* magazine and the *Advocacy for Animals* blog for Encyclopaedia Britannica, and has been published in *Utne Reader*, *One Green Planet* and several other publications, and has had essays published in *This I Believe: On Motherhood* (2012) and *Defiant Daughters: 21 Women on Art, Activism, Animals, and the Sexual Politics of Meat* (2013).

In 2012, Marla published her first novel, *The Adventures of Vivian Sharpe, Vegan Superhero* (**viviansharpe.com**), and in 2013, relaunched the web portal and magazine Vegan Street (**veganstreet.com**).

Made in the USA
Lexington, KY
15 February 2018